The Venetian Facade

The University of Notre Dame School of Architecture Series

RATIO ET ARCHITECTURA

The Venetian Facade
Michael Dennis
2024

Ratio et Architectura is a new book series from the School of Architecture at the University of Notre Dame. R & A is dedicated to scholarly research in architectural history and theory, professional projects and counter-projects, architectural pedagogy and the arts, architecture and the ecology, translation of important texts and treatises, and the documentation of important buildings. Michael Dennis's *The Venetian Facade* is the first book in the series.

The Venetian Facade

Michael Dennis

RATIO ET ARCHITECTURA
SCHOOL OF ARCHITECTURE . NOTRE DAME

ORO Editions
Publishers of Architecture, Art, and Design
Gordon Goff: Publisher

www.oroeditions.com
info@oroeditions.com

Published by ORO Editions

Author: Michael Dennis
Book Design: Michael Dennis
Project Manager: Jake Anderson

10 9 8 7 6 5 4 3 2 1 First Edition

ISBN: 978-1-961856-35-6

Prepress and Print work by ORO Editions Inc
Printed in China

ORO Editions makes a continuous effort to minimize the overall carbon footprint of its publications. As part of this goal, ORO, in association with Global ReLeaf, arranges to plant trees to replace those used in the manufacturing of the paper produced for its books. Global ReLeaf is an international campaign run by American Forests, one of the world's oldest nonprofit conservation organizations. Global ReLeaf is American Forests' education and action program that helps individuals, organizations, agencies, and corporations improve the local and global environment by planting and caring for trees.

Cover: Fantasy view of the Palazzo Grimani alongside the Ca' d'Oro

Acknowledgments

Living in Italy in the early 1960s was a period of focus on urbanism and Renaissance architecture and art, not Venice and Venetian facades; this occurred at Cornell in the 1970s. It is impossible to acknowledge one person or source. At that time it was simply a thing, part of the ongoing architectural discourse among the following faculty: Alan Chimacoff, Klaus Herdeg, Lee Hodgden, Fred Koetter, Colin Rowe, Werner Seligmann, John Shaw, Roger Sherwood, and Jerry Wells. Gradually, however, over many years and visits, Venice and the Venetian facade became an articulate "thing," resulting in this study. For recent reads, comments, encouragement, and suggestions, I thank Matt Bell, Alan Chimacoff, Randall Korman, John Ellis, Barbara Littenberg, Steven Peterson, and Jim Tice. All have been bombarded with various versions between release 1.0–13.0. Thanks especially to the University of Notre Dame School of Architecture for establishing this series and including this book. Finally, I want to thank my wife Christie, the best editor ever. There are three levels of editing: *structure*, *content*, and *copy*. Ideally, these should be sequential for obvious reasons. Editors should be able to focus primarily on copy editing—grammar, spelling, punctuation, consistency, etc. Life is not perfect, however, and stuff happens. Fortunately, Christie can distinguish between italic and Roman commas, and can spot every straight quotation mark instead of curly quotes. But she also understands ideas and the grammar and structure that supports them. Her reads and suggestions can be painful, but she is always correct. She has made this study far better—enough that she really should be considered a co-author.

Michael Dennis
Boston, MA
2024

For the memory of

Thomas L. Schumacher

and

for

Isabel and Serena,

Venete tutte e due

Palazzo Gritti Morosini, Campo Sant' Angelo

Contents

Preface

What? Yet another book about Venice? Why? There are hundreds of books about Venice: books about the history of Venice, cultural histories, specialty histories, and the history of Venetian architecture. For example, Deborah Howard's excellent book, *The Architectural History of Venice*, has a bibliography of 361 entries, and this is a highly selective list. There are also many guidebooks—some of which are useful—others never penetrating beyond "the facade has a certain charm," or "the pilaster strips give the composition an original flavor." There are even picture books of Venetian palace facades, variously covering family history, interiors, construction techniques, or period characteristics, but nothing about formal characteristics.

There are no books, however, that focus on the unique artistic characteristics of the Venetian facade and its potential relevance to contemporary architectural and urban issues, as this book intends. Why? One reason is that this requires a level of speculation outside the discipline of historiography. Another equally important reason is that "the facade" ceased to be an architectural consideration more than a century ago. Banished by modern architecture, the facade—as a simultaneous element of both architecture and urbanism—has become a lost art. It has been replaced by elaborate building configuration and narcissistic architectural invention. Even the word "facade" is enough to convince most modernists that they can smell the lingering odor of formaldehyde from the Beaux-Arts. Today, the facade is valued almost solely by practitioners of classicism—but even they neglect the Venetian facade.

Architectural education has also avoided the issue of the facade by focusing on *the concept*, or *elaborate configuration*, or *the theoretical idea* ("I think this project is under-theorized"). During the 1970s at Cornell, however, much attention was given to the idea of the facade, especially the Venetian facade. It was part of the ongoing discourse, both in history/theory classes and design studios. In the intervening years, however, the idea and the art of the facade has become even more remote, as architecture has become increasingly narcissistic and anti-urban. This has enabled the plan and, more recently, the 3D digital image to occupy center stage in practice and academia.

This book is about architecture. It is not about history, although a bit of history is necessary to set the context. It is not about theory, although, again, a bit is necessary to connect the facade with urbanism. It is also not about structure and technology. And, most definitely, it is not about *the plan*. All of these topics are well-covered elsewhere. This book is about *the facade*. It explores the art and typology of the Venetian facade, not only as a high point of architectural literacy and achievement, but as a potentially useful contemporary stimulant.

A word of explanation regarding terminology. Technically, there is only one *palazzo* in Venice, the Palazzo Ducale (Doge's Palace); a residential building is a *casa*, or *ca'*, as in the Ca' d'Oro. There is also only one *piazza* in Venice, the Piazza San Marco; an urban square in Venice is a *campo*, as in the Campo San Polo. In contemporary usage, however, this system is less strict, and *palazzo* (palace) is often substituted for *casa*. Both are used in this book. Finally, in this book, *The Venetian Facade* does not refer to all facades, but primarily to Venetian *palace* facades.

View in Venice, on the Grand Canal (Rialto Bridge), Canaletto, 1734

View of San Marco, *The Bacino di San Marco on Ascension Day*, Canaletto, 1733–34

'Veneziani Gran Signori'

To arrive in Venice from the hard Italian cities of stone—Milano, Bologna, Firenze, Roma—is to be confounded. All the standard urban elements are absent: the fortified palaces of giant rusticated stones, the remnants of Roman grids, the fragments of fortification walls, and the previously pedestrian streets overloaded with contemporary traffic. Thus, even to the trained architectural mind, Venice is mesmerizing but incomprehensible. Everything is different. It is soft, irregular, and colorful, and its very seductiveness tends to deflect rational thought. For example, the similar but infinitely varied facades all deny principles of gravity. Penetrating this fantastical world requires a different than normal approach. To state the obvious: Venice is unique, and its uniqueness has deep roots.

The uniqueness of Venice, especially its facades, is primarily due to two factors. The most significant factor is the circumstance of the city's foundation; its founders were Roman, but it is not a Roman founded town. The other factor is the city's historic relationship to Byzantium rather than Rome.

Of the many things that contribute to the uniqueness of Venice, however, the conundrum of the presence of classicism may be the most curious, interesting, and problematic. It can be argued, for example—and it is a fundamental thesis of this book—the classical facades are the least interesting Venetian facades, and classicism tends to overshadow and obscure the more interesting aspects of Venice. Just as Haussmann's Boulevards mask the virtues of eighteenth-century Paris, the classical civic structure of the Piazza San Marco and the monumental classical houses of the Grand Canal deflect attention from the varied richness of Venice's urban fabric. It is no accident that every guide book for Venice begins with the Piazza San Marco and the Grand Canal. They are, indeed, among the world's most beautiful squares and "streets," and together with the *scuole* and the Palladian churches, they loom large in the image and memory of Venice.

Venice was not a Roman founded city, however, so after some eight hundred years of non-classical urban and architectural development, what explains the importation of classicism into Venice? Why? And, why are Veneziani "gran signori"? The roots of the answer, as well as the answer to Venice's uniqueness, lie in the city's origins and in the pre-Venetian history of Italy and the Veneto.

Veneziani gran signori
Padovani gran Dottore
Vicentini magna gatti
Veronese tutti matti [1]

Opposite page: Grand Canal

1

VENETO–BYZANTINE
Ca' Loredan, early 13th century

Fondaco dei Turchi, late 12th century

GOTHIC
Ca' d'Oro, begun 1421

Doge's Palace, south wing begun 1341

EARLY RENAISSANCE
Ca' Dario, 1487–92

Palazzo Contarini Dal Zaffo, ca. 1490

RENAISSANCE
Palazzo Corner–Spinelli, ca. 1490
Mauro Codussi

Palazzo Vendramin Calergi, begun ca 1502
Mauro Codussi

ROMAN RENAISSANCE
Palazzo Grimani, 1556–75
Michele Sanmicheli

Palazzo Corner, begun ca. 1545
Jacopo Sansovino

BAROQUE
Ca' Rezzonico, ca. 1667
Baldassare Longhena

Ca' Pesaro, begun ca. 1562
Baldassare Longhena

NEOCLASSICAL
Palazzo Giustinian Michiel Alvise, 17th century

Palazzo Michiel dalle Colonne, 1697
Antonio Gaspari

The spectacle of Venice afforded some hours of astonishment and some days of disgust. Old and in general ill-built houses, ruined pictures, and stinking ditches dignified with the pompous denomination of canals; a fine bridge spoilt by two rows of houses on it, and a large square decorated with the worst architecture I ever saw.

Edward Gibbon,
Memoires

Introduction

The Venetian Palace is to the art of the facade as the French Hôtel is to the art of the plan—the quintessential level of architectural achievement. Unique in the history of architecture, and a product of an equally unique circumstance, the Venetian facade spread to the Italian mainland and has inspired modern facades as well.

The Venetian facade offered possibilities of infinite variation, and thus not only sustained consistent development in Venice for over seven hundred years, but also provided Venice with its mesmerizing combination of variety and unity. Almost modern in its planar abstraction and lack of structural expression, the Venetian facade utilizes the same formal compositional principles found in French Hôtel plans, namely, asymmetry, re-centering, and local symmetry. It was these principles that contributed to the sophistication of Venetian facade development despite the diagrammatic simplicity of the basic plan and facade type.

Many cities of the Italian mainland—such as Florence—grew out of the Roman Empire. They had grid plans and architecture that developed out of classicism. Venice, however, developed differently. Its origins were not Roman. Its plan was irregular, and its architecture was not classical. A seafaring merchant city, Venice's orientation was always to the East and Byzantium rather than Rome and the mainland.

Venice was an independent republic for 1,100 years—from its first Doge in 697 to its submission to Napoleon in 1797—and did not become part of Italy until 1866.

This, together with the location and characteristics of its site, are fundamental to its urban and architectural development.

Venice is a Gothic, or Byzantine, city, not a classical city. Classicism, with its structurally representative grids, is a "foreign language" that arrived in Venice in the late fifteenth century, effectively numbing the oriental tapestry-like characteristics of the Gothic facade, which had reached a high point of development before the arrival of classicism. In fact, it can be argued that Venice's relatively modest amount of domestic classical architecture is, with some notable exceptions, the city's least interesting architecture and somewhat at odds with the rest of Venice's architecture. Neoclassical facades, however, returned to a simpler, more abstract language and thus renewed the vitality of the Venetian facade.

Most books about Venice and Venetian architecture are history books organized chronologically around canonical works. This book is about design, so chronology is of secondary importance, but an abbreviated chronological overview of Venetian periods and facades might provide a useful framework because many of the most stimulating Venetian facades do not appear in history books.

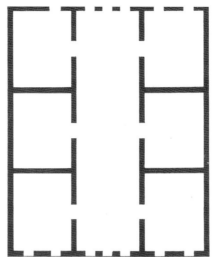

1. Plan diagram of a tripartite Venetian house

2. The two bay types of a Venetian facade

The Venetian Facade

The word "facade" basically means "face." It descends from the Latin, *facia*, to the Italian, *faccia* (face) and *facciata* (facade), and finally to the French, *façade*. The word has two basic meanings, which Webster defines as: 1) "The front of a building, also any face of a building given special architectural treatment;" and 2) "A false, superficial, or artificial appearance or effect."

The Venetian facade is planar, centralized, and has no structural indication of loads being carried to the ground (or water). Indeed, it is a "free-facade," more like an oriental tapestry that often appears as though it hangs from the cornice, rather than being supported from below. It is composed of two bay types, a central bay with large openings and a side bay with a blank panel between widely spaced windows. A "typical" Venetian facade consists of three bays related to a three-bay plan.

Figure/field principles and local symmetries are fundamental to Venetian facades. The gridded "field," or fabric, of the facade may not always be overt, but it is always present and related to the size of the human body. The "figures" that emerge from the fabric of the facade are always visible, however. They are locally symmetrical and may relate to the regulating lines of the field, or they may be independent.

Often, multiple figural readings are possible due to details and proportional relationships. In the case of Palazzo Clary, the figural reading of the grouped center windows and balcony on the *piano nobile* tends to jump the gap of narrow wall surface to absorb the flanking vertical windows as well as the high mezzanine windows below to make an enlarged rectangular figure, or dominant "spot." The arched windows above this expanded figure tend to expand the spot still further. The arched windows near the outer edges of the facade function to stretch it into a taught membrane. Finally, the two outer balconies on the *piano nobile* reinforce this reading because they relate to the central balcony, not its two flanking windows. The Palazzo Clary facade is symmetrical, but local symmetries play a bigger role when the facade is not symmetrical, as with the Ca' D'Oro.

Figure/field principles are also important for the secondary elements of the facade, such as windows. For example, the outer third-floor windows of this house are clearly figural elements that seem to float, isolated and without balconies, on the surface of the wall, locked in to the implied grid of the facade only by their vertical and horizontal alignment. On the piano nobile, however, the central and outer edge windows have aggressive balconies which stretch and extend their vertical characteristics, thus connecting them to the high mezzanine windows below, providing a larger, expanded figural reading. The idea of extending the reading of windows and balconies by frames, panels, balconies, string courses, etc. makes the grids of many Venetian facades much more prominent, thereby resulting in a more subtle figure/field relationship with multiple readings.

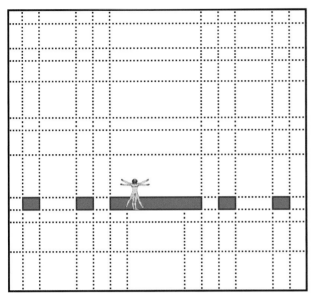

1. Palazzo Clary, regulating lines of the field

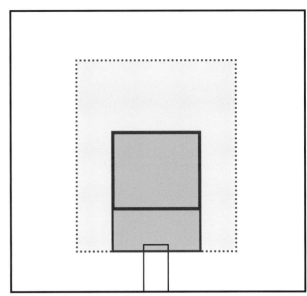

2. Palazzo Clary, primary figures

3. Palazzo Clary

1. Greek temple at Paestum

The Classical Facade

In contrast to the planar Venetian facade, with no structural indication of loads being carried to the ground (or water), the gridded plasticity and lateral emphasis of classical facades is about loads being carried to the ground, either by structural columns or by load-bearing walls with superimposed representation of structure.

Facade as Figure or Field

The principle of figure versus field describes two different types of facade: figurative, centralized facades like the pediment—the face—of a Greek temple and lateral facades without figural emphasis, like the sides of a Greek temple. The Greeks used the Doric column as what it was, a structural load-bearing element of temples and stoas.

The Greeks rarely made architectural walls. As the Romans expanded the repertoire of civic buildings, however, they developed systems of engaged columns and entablatures to represent structure and to order the walls of their buildings and cities.

With the full invasion of classicism into Venice in the sixteenth century, field replaced figure and plasticity replaced planar

2. Temple of Bacchus, Baalbek, 2nd c. BC

surface. The facade of the Palazzo Corner della Ca' Grande by Jacopo Sansovino, for example, has a fairly even distribution of windows and superimposed columnar order laterally across the facade, thereby suppressing the traditional Venetian tripartite facade typology. The expression of the central portego bay is very faint, and the horizontal entablatures tend to erase even that trace. The paired columns and the rusticated base also suppress the planar quality of the wall in favor of a robust Roman classical plasticity.

1. Temple of Hera II, Paestum, 6th c. BC

2. Palazzo Corner della Ca' Grande, 16th c., Sansovino

Three Facade Types

Facades can be seen as *Mask*, *Mediator*, or *Membrane*. To some degree these three types are chronological.

Renaissance and Baroque facades are usually the first type, facade as mask.[3] These facades are heavy, fortress-like walls with relatively small openings, no balconies, and little to no relationship with the plan, as with the Palazzo Farnese in Rome.

Venetian facades and Parisian boulevard facades are the second type, facade as mediator. These facades are more "porous" with larger windows, balconies, and a more open relationship to the plan. Balconies play a major role in making a discrete, occupiable link between the private interior and the public exterior realm. Details can even extend the reading of windows, making the openness seem greater than it actually is.

Modern facades, such as those of Le Corbusier, are the third type, facade as membrane. It is the modern columnar structural frame that enables the facade as membrane.[4] This is the penultimate step in the opening up of the interior to the exterior, the last step being the abandonment of the facade in favor of so-called curtain walls of glass—and with it the abandonment and eventual demise of the city.

Facade as Mask

Renaissance and Baroque facades, like masks, began as defensive walls and became displays of power and prestige, with more allegiance to the public realm than the private. They were the facades of streets and squares.

The Palazzo Farnese in Rome is an elegant example. The facade has a significant amount of surface, as window openings are small. String courses mark the floor lines, and the windows are evenly distributed across the facade, masking a very large, double-story room in the upper left-hand corner of the facade, the fifty-nine foot high Sala di Ercole.[5] The adjacent image is a fantasy speculation of what might have happened if Michele Sanmicheli had finished Sangallo's palazzo rather than Michelangelo.

1. Palazzo Farnese, with location of Sala di Ercole, Rome, Giulio Sangallo and Michelangelo

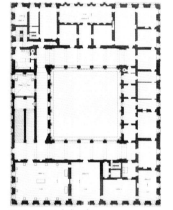

2. Piano Nobile plan

3. Sala di Ercole

4. Fantasy facade alla Michele Sanmicheli

1. Palazzo Corner-Mocenigo, Venice, Michele Sanmicheli

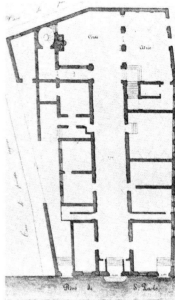

2. Palazzo Corner-Mocenigo, ground plan

Facade as Mediator

While the regularity of the Renaissance facade trumped everything—even fifty-nine foot high double height-spaces—Venetian palace facades were more open and reflective of the private realm. These facades always have a general relationship with the plan, i.e., the side bays to the rooms and the center bay to the portego, but not always a literal one. The plans are often irregular due to local urban conditions. For example, the plan of the Palazzo Corner-Mocenigo has an irregular perimeter, but the portego establishes a regular center, and the facade adheres strictly to the tripartite ideal model of the Venetian facade.

Unlike most Italian palaces, Venetian balconies allow the windows to extend to the floor, like French doors or windows. This automatically creates more openness as well as a more intimate relationship between inside and outside, like Parisian apartment building windows. This would lead to greater integration in the eighteenth century and the *promenade architecturale*, to accompany the *promenade du boulevard*.

3. *Man on a Balcony, Boulevard Haussmann*, Gustave Caillbotte, 1880

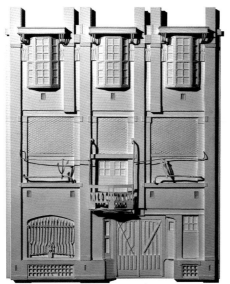

1. Facade model of the house of Dr. Van Neck

2. House of Dr. Van Neck, Brussels, 1912, Antoine Pompe

Frame and Facade

The point-load structural frame's replacement of the load-bearing structural wall represents the most revolutionary change in the history of architecture.[6]

The structural frame emerged in the late nineteenth century, but its possibilities had stirred theoretical debates at Paris's École des Beaux-Arts for decades before. The argument was essentially one of "beauty" versus "truth." Truth, as represented by the possibilities of iron and steel construction, held the possibility of "honest expression" (and industrialized allure), but beauty held fast at the École until almost the Second World War.

In the first half of the twentieth century, American architects—mostly educated at the École des Beaux-Arts—utilized the steel frame embedded in masonry for both low and tall buildings. "Beauty" trumped "truth;" facades were still made.

One early-modern European example of both frame and facade is the 1912 House of Doctor Van Neck by Antoine Pompe. The facade is a combination of structural grid and a high degree of three-dimensional modeling. It is idiosyncratic enough, however, to make a mannerist architect, like Giulio Romano, blush with envy.

Organizationally, the structure describes a nine-square grid with a narrow central bay and wider side bays—the opposite of a typical Venetian facade. One of the column lines does not carry to the ground, however, and the double entry doors are centered on this column line. An ornate balcony re-establishes the authority of the compressed central bay, but appears to slip down below the apparent floor line, hanging perilously close to the entry doors below.

The vertical "pilasters" of the frame totally dominate the horizontals, which emphasizes the verticality of the bays, yet there is no sense of weight being carried to the ground. Indeed, in spite of the high-relief plasticity, the facade seems to hang from the top, like a Venetian facade. This is due to the three bay windows on the top floor, appearing to hang from very large, projecting eyelids with nothing below the windows except three architectural "beauty marks." The outside windows are asymmetrical within their bays, but are re-centered by stub pilasters that also seem to hang rather than support. On the middle floor, there are small, secondary pilasters that appear to support a steel lintel over the grills, resting on horizontal projecting trays, but they contribute to the continuity of surface. This is a remarkable facade that is at once facade and frame—with no classical elements.

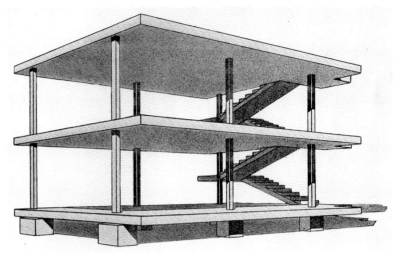

1. The Domino Frame, Le Corbusier, 1914

Facade as Membrane

Le Corbusier's Domino Frame is the most iconic idea of one strain of modernism, that which grew out of Paris and Cubism. Unlike the Chicago steel frame, which was omni-directional, the Domino Frame was concrete, and, in contrast to the vertical dominance of load-bearing walls, the horizontal slabs were dominant. In essence, this meant that the facade was unnecessary.

Indeed, Mies' 1929 Barcelona Pavilion defined one continuous space between horizontal slabs. There were literally no facades. The building was not an isolated object but an architectural event along a major processional sequence.

Like the Barcelona Pavilion, the villa at Garches was an architectural component of an extended sequence, one which began at the entry gate, extended through the building, and ended in the garden, or the roof terrace. In contrast, Le Corbusier provided a sophisticated facade for the Villa Stein-de Monzie even though, theoretically, one was not needed. He provided a facade as membrane, complete with opaque surfaces, projections, and receding spaces, making explicit that the facade was not supported on the ground but rather was hung from the frame. In other words, a facade was needed, even when not structurally necessary.

2. The Villa Stein-de Monzie, Garches, 1927, Le Corbusier

3. The Barcelona Pavilion, 1929, Mies Van der Rohe

Aerial view of urban fabric between the Frari and Campo San Polo

Aerial view of Venice

Venezia: *Forma Urbis*

The urban form of Venice comprises consistent urban fabric and a legible civic structure, but both the civic structure and the urban fabric are much less regular and clear than the typical Italian city.

Civic Structure

If the civic structure of a city is a legible sequence of public spaces and important buildings, in Venice that structure would be Piazza San Marco, the Grand Canal, the Rialto, and the train station. That sequence is readily legible in both plan and reality. Because it is so strong, however, it tends to mask the rich, surrounding urban fabric of small streets, canals, and spaces.

Urban Fabric

In contrast to the regular grids and spaces of Roman founded towns such as Florence, Venice's urban islands, or neighborhoods, developed incrementally from the natural irregularity of the Venetian Lagoon—each with a campo, a well, a church, and irregular urban fabric.

Henry Miller described the continuity of going from one neighborhood to another in Paris as being like passing through a series of invisible beaded curtains, whereas in the sixteenth century, Francesco Sansovino (Jacopo Sansovino's

son) described going from one neighborhood to another in Venice as being like passing from one town to another.

Indeed, each Venetian neighborhood is like an irregular version of an ideal town with a clear center and consistent urban fabric but, less often, a clear edge. Thus, Venice's neighborhoods are infinitely varied and formally illusive, making the whole city of these neighborhoods mesmerizing and seemingly incomprehensible.

The urban form of Venice is medieval; there are no set-piece boulevards and no Platonic-shaped squares. All of Venice's public spaces, including the Piazza San Marco, are picturesque and irregular, as is their surrounding urban fabric. Aside from the Piazza San Marco, the only designed, unified spaces in Venice are the cloisters of monasteries.

Neighborhood campi, may have one or more beautiful palazzi, but they are generally low-key, informal, and unpretentious spaces. The campi are the living rooms of their respective neighborhoods, and are full of activities that change throughout the day. They are also the playgrounds for children.

1. View of the Venetian Lagoon

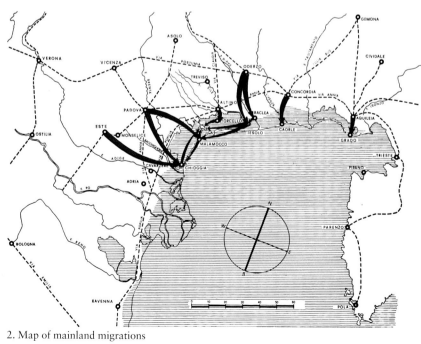

2. Map of mainland migrations

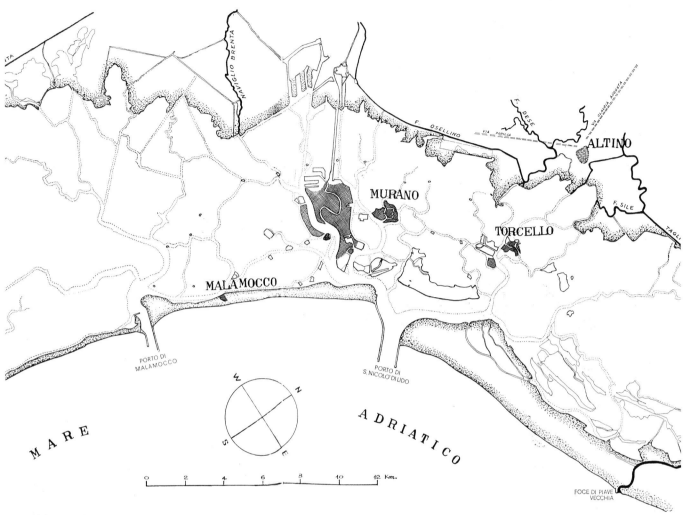

Map of the Venetian Lagoon

Origins

The form of Venice and the Venetian house both grew out of their location in the Venetian Lagoon, a shallow body of brackish water concealing a dense, irregular pattern of subsurface canals.[1]

Between the sixth and eighth centuries, residents of the Roman coastal centers of the Veneto had fled the mainland to escape Barbarian invasions and established themselves on the sandy islands of the lagoon. In 737, the city administration was moved from Malamocco to Rialto (now Venice), and was established as the administrative center of the region. In 828, St. Mark was adopted as the patron saint of the city.

Until the city surrendered to Napoleon in 1797, the Republic of Venice—*La Serenissima*—was never conquered. The city's location in the center of the lagoon served as a natural and impenetrable defense. Even Napoleon's cannons could not reach Venice from the mainland; ships entering the mouth of the lagoon were subject to destruction by a Venetian fortress overlooking the mouth, or they ran aground in the maze of unseen canals known only to the Venetians. This defense system allowed Venice an internal openness unavailable to mainland cities like Florence and Rome.

1. The Venetian Lagoon

2. 7th century Venice

3. 9th century Venice

4. 11th century Venice

5. 20th century Venice

Foundation of Venice

In 811, the doge Agnello Participazio (811–27), moved with the regional administration to the islands of Rialto, and the future city of Venice began to be permanently established on the scattered islands in the center of the lagoon.[2]

Originally, communication among the islands was only by boat, but over time, canals were filled and bridges were built until the city was densely settled with a dual circulation system via water and land.

Three things were required to sustain life there: safety, food, and water. Safety was provided by the lagoon; fish provided a limited, but healthy diet; while water was ubiquitous, it was brackish and undrinkable. Thus, the crucial detail that allowed sustainable development was a system of wells to provide drinking water.

The irregular urban islands were organized around a field, or *campo*, each with a church and a well. The resulting neighborhoods could have survived without a church or campo, but not without a well. The Venetian wells captured rainwater, filtered it through sand, and stored it in brick-lined wells, which occurred in courtyards as well as campi.

1. Aerial view of Campo San Polo

2. Venetian well

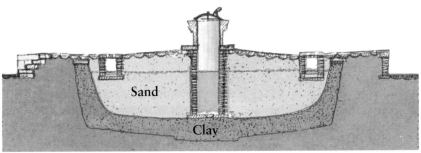

3. Venetian well, section

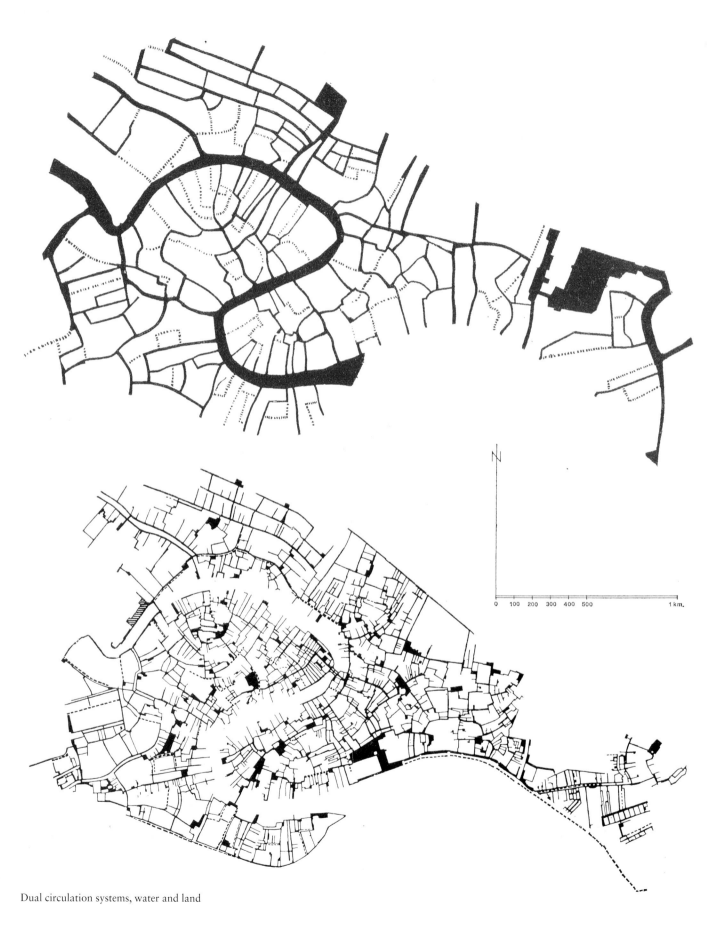

Dual circulation systems, water and land

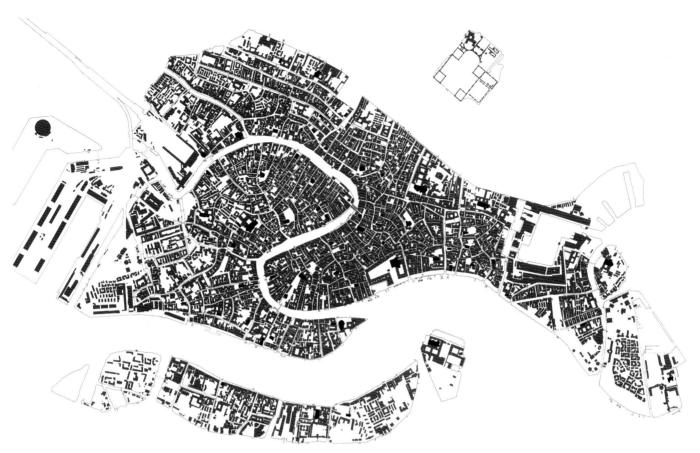

1. Plan of Venice's built fabric

Dual Circulation Systems

Just as the well was the urban element that allowed sustainable life within the lagoon, the arched bridge was the urban element that allowed the simultaneous functioning of two complete circulation systems—water and land.

Most of the bridges in Venice are single arch bridges, but as seen in Bellini's painting, there are some triple-arch bridges. There are endless plan configurations of connections, but more importantly, they are spectacular viewing platforms.

2. *Miracle of the Cross at the Bridge of San Lorenzo*, Gentile Bellini, ca. 1500

3. Single-arch bridge

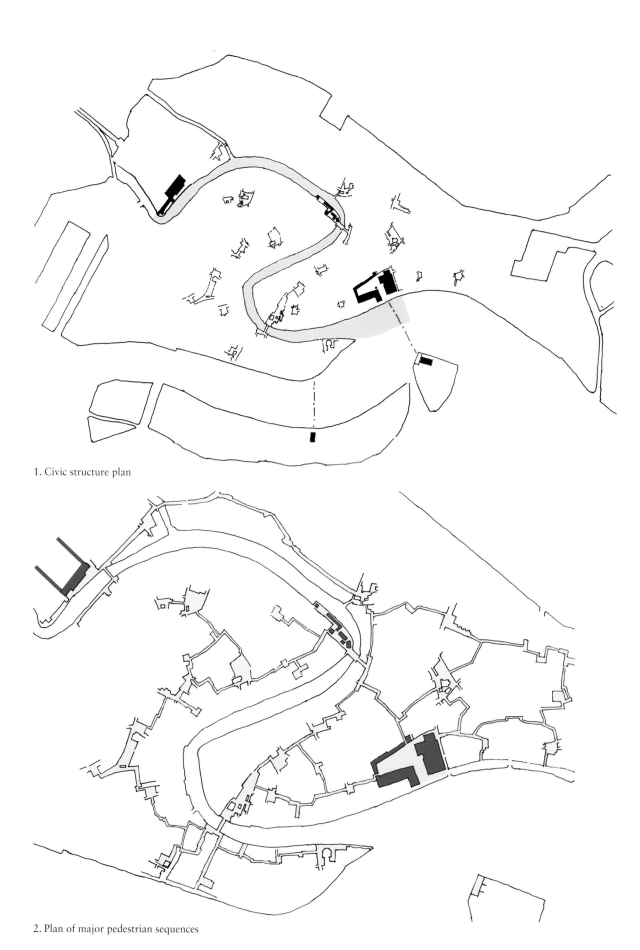

1. Civic structure plan

2. Plan of major pedestrian sequences

1. Aerial view of Grand Canal

Civic Structure and Urban Fabric

The primary civic structure—indeed, the only legible civic structure—of Venice is the Grand Canal and the sequence of San Marco, Rialto, and Santa Lucia. The lack of secondary civic structure, beyond the Grand Canal, and perhaps the Giudecca, is due to the development of Venice's urban fabric.

As the original islands grew and became connected by bridges, discontinuities within and between the islands were inevitable. The resulting complexities and discontinuities make the city incomprehensible to the uninitiated. No town planner/urban designer could have designed such an intricate, complicated urban pattern. Only natural, incremental development could produce such a plan.

If each neighborhood has a clear center surrounded by dense urban fabric, none have a clear edge except those facing major canals. Even then it is difficult to tell when one neighborhood, or *sestiere*, ends and another begins. The Piazza San Marco neighborhood is the most forceful example of this.

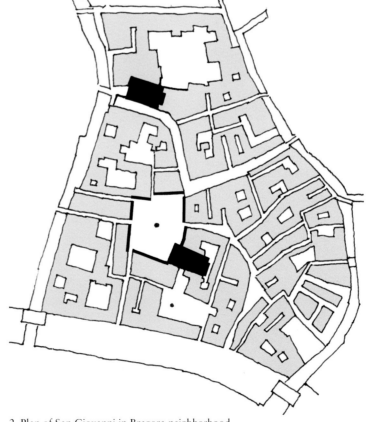

2. Plan of San Giovanni in Bragora neighborhood

1. *Reception of the French Ambassador in Venice*, Canaletto, 1727

The Grand Canal

In most Italian cities the core of the civic structure is a piazza. In Venice the civic structure consists of one of the world's grandest "streets," the Grand Canal. As Venice's "Main Street," the Grand Canal connects important palaces as well as the two contemporary entrances to Venice, the Piazza San Marco and the Santa Lucia Railway Station.

For centuries, the Piazza San Marco was the sole public face of the city and the entrance from the sea—serving both fishermen and important visiting dignitaries. Today, the Santa Lucia Railway Station on the back side of the city serves as the main entrance for the thousands of daily tourists.

The Grand Canal is the Grand Theater of Venice's pageantry, confirming the openness of facades and the enduring role of Venice's unique balconies.

2. Santa Lucia Train Station

1. *Venice: the Grand Canal from the Palazzo Dolfin-Manin to the Rialto Bridge*, Canaletto, ca. 1740–50

2. *The Mouth of the Grand Canal looking West towards the Carita*, Canaletto, 1729

1. Doge's Compound
2. Chapel
3. Harbor
4. St. Mark's
5. Rio Batario
6. San Geminiano
7. Piazza San Marco
8. Procuratie Vecchie
9. Piazzetta
10. Two Columns

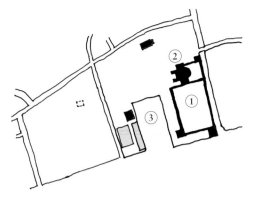

1. Piazza San Marco, plan, 9th–11th c.

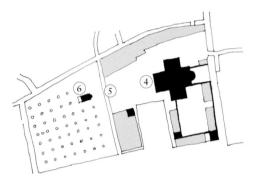

2. Piazza San Marco, plan, 12th c.

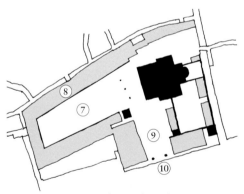

3. Piazza San Marco, plan, 12th–13th c.

Piazza San Marco

It took a thousand years to build the Piazza San Marco, Venice's only designed, unified urban composition.

Unlike unified squares such as the Place Vendôme in Paris, or the Place Stanislas in Nancy, which were designed and built for kings in a relatively short period of time, the Piazza San Marco was built incrementally by a republic.[3]

In 811, Agnello Participazio settled on the island site that would later become the Doge's Palace and the church of St. Mark's. The doge soon made a fortified compound on the side facing the Grand Canal, and a small wooden church, the doge's chapel, was attached. The harbor reached almost to the chapel.

Almost three centuries later, in 1094, the rebuilt cruciform church of St. Mark's was completed. The area in front of the church remained undeveloped, and the site across the Rio Batario to the west contained the small church of San Geminiano in an orchard owned by the Nuns of San Zaccaria.

The major formation of the piazza began around 1150. The Procuratie Vecchie (the building for the Procurators, or managers, of St. Marks) was begun as a uniform two-story colonnaded building with ground floor shops along the north side of the square in 1172. Two columns were also placed in the Piazzetta in 1172. The 1496 Gentile Bellini painting below illustrates the piazza three centuries later.

4. *Corpus Domini Procession in St. Marks*, Gentile Bellini, 1496

1. *Piazza San Marco*, Canaletto, 1720s

Bellini's painting is a last image of the square before its major renaissance remodeling during the early 1500s. Canaletto's two views from the 1720s (above) and 1739 (below), show the piazza in its nominally complete condition. Only the western enclosure, with the church of San Geminiano, would later be changed by Napoleon.

The new three-story Procuratie Vecchie began in 1513 and the Procuratie Nuove, built between 1503–1660, were moved back to expose the campanile and provide a better perspective of San Marco.

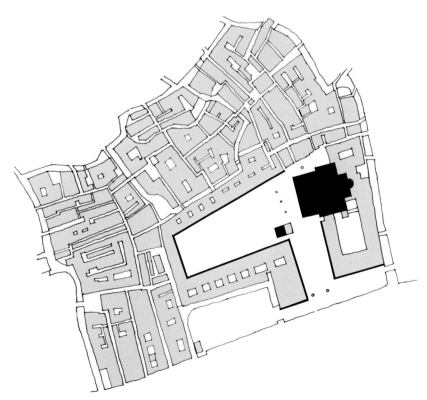

2. *Piazza San Marco*, Canaletto, 1739

3. Piazza San Marco, plan

1. S. Maria Formosa, side facade

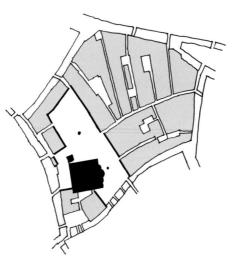

2. Campo S. Maria Formosa neighborhood, plan

3. Campo S. Maria Formosa neighborhood, aerial view

4. *View of Campo S. Maria Formosa*, Canaletto, ca. 1730

5. Campo S. Maria Formosa toward Palazzo Priuli-Ruzzini

Campo S. Maria Formosa

The campo of this island neighborhood is a large, rectangular space defined by a series of important palazzi. The focus of the space is the spectacular church of Santa Maria Formosa by Mauro Codussi (except the facades). The church is at an odd angle to the campo, creating smaller squares around it, one of which frames the side entrance facade. The other side has three rounded apses bulging into the campo. These accentuate the figurative form of the church, activating the space. This, along with the campanile, is a characteristic form of several Venetian campi.

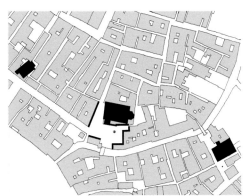

1. Campo SS. Apostoli neighborhood, plan

2. Campo SS. Apostoli, aerial view

3. *View of Campo SS. Apostoli*, Canaletto, ca. 1730

Campo SS. Apostoli

Analogous to S. Maria Formosa, this church, its chapels (the domed one attributed to Mauro Codussi), and campanile form a figural complex that defines a series of smaller squares around it. Because of its location midway on the primary route between the train station and Piazza San Marco, it is a very active but casual urban space, with shops and restaurants. The thirteenth-century Palazzo Falier closes the campo along the rio and leads to San Marco. All routes out of the campo lead to interesting sequences of campi.

4. Campo SS. Apostoli

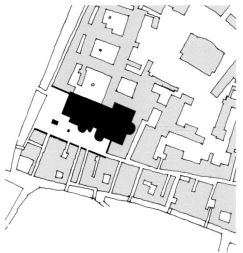

1. Campo SS. Giovanni e Paolo neighborhood, plan

2. Campo SS. Giovanni e Paolo, aerial view

3. Campo SS. Giovanni e Paolo

4. *View of Campo SS. Giovanni e Paolo*, Canaletto, 1735–38

5. View of Campo SS. Giovanni e Paolo

Campo SS. Giovanni e Paolo

Unlike the Campo Santa Maria Formosa, the Campo SS. Giovanni Paolo, or in Venetian dialect, *Zanipolo*, is not a space defined by important palazzi. Rather, it is an "L"-shaped space, the quality of which comes from the church of Giovanni and Paolo, its bulging side chapels, and by the remarkable facade of the Scuola Grande di San Marco (now the Ospedali). Verrocchio's superb equestrian statue of Bartolomeo Colleoni articulates the front rectangular space from the side space activated by the rounded sculptural chapels. The dueling facades are astonishing.

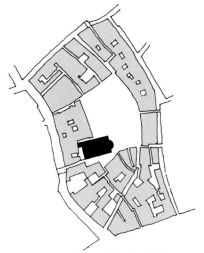

1. Campo S. Polo neighborhood, plan

2. Campo S. Polo, aerial view

3. *View of Campo S. Polo*, Canaletto

Campo S. Polo

One of the largest campi in Venice, the Campo S. Polo, is not dominated by a church, nor does the church noticeably contribute to the quality of the urban space. There are several excellent palazzi, however, including the Palazzo Soranzo, the Palazzo Maffetti-Tiepolo, and the rear facade of the Palazzo Corner-Mocenigo by Michele Sanmicheli. The church actually faces away from the campo and plays only a small role in the quality of the space. Nevertheless, the campo is a very active space, as a link between the Rialto Market and the Accademia.

4. Campo S. Polo

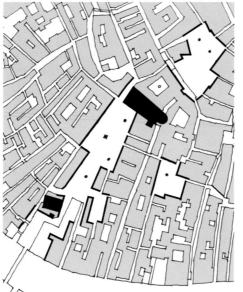

1. Campo S. Stefano and S. Angelo neighborhood, plan

2. Campo S. Stefano, aerial view

3. *Campo S. Angelo*, Canaletto, ca. 1730

4. *View of Campo S. Stefano*, Bernardo Belotto, 1740

5. View of Campo S. Stefano toward the Palazzo Loredan

Campi S. Stefano and S. Angelo

The location of the Campo S. Angelo and the Campo Santo Stefano is an important link on the route from the train station, and the route from San Marco to the Accademia, which ensures that the Campo S. Stefano is active at all hours of the day. The Campo S. Angelo is defined by important palazzi and the campanile of the church of S. Stefano. The Campo S. Stefano also has important palazzi, including the Palazzo Loredan and the adjacent Palazzo Pisani.

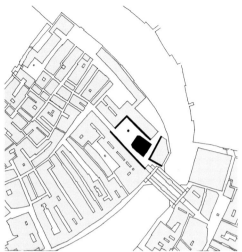

1. Campo di Rialto neighborhood, plan

2. Rialto markets, aerial view

3. Rialto markets, aerial view

4. *View of S. Giacomo di Rialto*, Canaletto, 1726

Campo S. Giacomo di Rialto

This is the only purely rectangular campo in Venice. Surrounded by arcades, the space focuses on the church of S. Giacomo di Rialto. The campo is the center of the city's extensive market complex, an elaborate urban combination of buildings and spaces stretching along the Grand Canal from the Rialto Bridge to the fish market. Densely populated due to its function and location, this area is the front door to the San Polo district.

5. *View of Campo di Rialto*, Canaletto, 1760

Detail of library facade, Piazza San Marco, Jacopo Sansovino

What are you classical columns doing here in London?
Why sir, we don't quite know.

Mythical passerby to the facade of Inigo Jones's
Queen's Banqueting House, begun 1619, and the columns' supposed response

The Classical Facade

The Italian Renaissance invasion into the medieval cultures of France and England arrived late, ca. 1550 in France and ca. 1600 in England. In France, medieval resistance to classicism produced a hybrid language for over a century, but in England the entrance of classicism was pure and abrupt—hence the above question to the columns of the Queen's Banqueting House.

One could ask the same question of the white classical columns in Venice: *What are you doing here in Venice*?

Gothic architecture had never completely succeeded in mainland Italy as it had in France, Germany, and England, but by the end of the fifteenth century it had reached a high point of development in Venice.

The Renaissance emerged in Florence in the early fifteenth century. Brunelleschi's Foundling Hospital was built 1419–27, the same period as the famous Venetian Gothic house, the Ca' d'Oro (1428).

Unlike Florence and Rome, Venice was oriented toward the East and was resistant to change to more Western influence. Nevertheless, by the 1480s, early Renaissance architecture by Mauro Codussi and others began appearing in Venice.

It was the sack of Rome in 1527 that precipitated a major change in Venetian architecture and produced the fantasy of Venice as the "New Rome." Jacopo Sansovino fled Rome for Venice; around the same time, the Veronese architect Michele Sanmicheli returned from central Italy; and Sebastiano Serlio came to Venice from Bologna.

The fantasy of a connection to a Roman past facilitated the substitution of a robust Roman plasticity for the planarity of the early Renaissance. White Istrian stone replaced brick and plaster as the primary building material, marking a sea-change in Venetian urbanism and domestic architecture. In the early years of the sixteenth century, grids of classical columns and entablatures engaged the facades of both public and private buildings. The Piazza San Marco was the recipient of a major renovation effort by Sansovino, with the new, repetitive architecture rolled out like urban wallpaper.

Due to the power of the Piazza San Marco and the classical palaces of the Grand Canal, Venice might appear to be a classical city to the contemporary tourist hitting the high spots of a two day visit. This classical image not only absorbs attention away from superb non-classical architecture, but it also deflects attention from a surprising amount of more prosaic architecture—the vernacular buildings of Venice.

Oddly, it may be a useful prelude to begin a discussion of Venetian facades with what the most interesting Venetian facades are not—classical facades.

33

1. Palazzo Medici-Riccardi, Florence

2. View of San Marco with Doge's Palace

3. View of San Marco with Pitti Palace

Doge's Palace

Florence vs. Venice

Florence and the other stone cities of the Italian mainland were subject to violence from within and their architectural form reflects that. The Renaissance palaces of Florence, for example, are like fortifications with rusticated ground floors and small openings. The massive exterior wall of the Palazzo Medici-Riccardi gives a sense of great loads being carried to the ground by the three floors, which begin with heavy rustication on the ground floor and get lighter as they rise to the cornice. The only controllable exterior space is the building's courtyard.

Thanks to the safety provided by the lagoon the architecture of Venice is lighter, whiter, more planar, and—especially—more open. Exterior public space flows into the buildings; balconies proliferate, and despite exposed columns, there is no sense of structural load being carried to the ground. Indeed, the exterior of the Doge's Palace is like an upside-down version of the Palazzo Medici-Riccardi, with the solid on top and the most opening on the ground floor.[1] (The Pitti Palace in Venice in lieu of the Doge's Palace, for example, would be unimaginable.)

1. Palazzo Medici-Riccardi, 1444, Florence, Michelozzo

2. Palazzo Rucellai, Florence, Alberti, 1446–51

Renaissance Classicism

The birth of the Renaissance in fifteenth-century Florence marks the reemergence of the classical language of architecture and, most importantly, its application to private urban buildings, namely the Renaissance Palazzo.

Two models may be considered the Adam and Eve of all future classical urban buildings: the Palazzo Medici (1444), with a three-story facade of graded rustication and the Palazzo Rucellai (1446–51), with a grid of "engaged" pilasters to order the facade, the first building since antiquity to do so. Most Florentine palaces, and the two-story Roman versions, were detached, or semi-detached, block-like buildings, but they were at once conspicuous and part of the urban fabric. Few were pure party-wall buildings.

The facade of the Palazzo Rucellai is very shallow, but it introduced the ideas of phenomenal layering, implied perspective, and proportional relationships within a relatively flat picture plane. This led to future exploitations of greater depth, more complicated layers, and the use of giant orders to unify the facade vertically.

3. Palazzo Rucellai, bay detail

Michelangelo's Palazzo dei Conservatori on Rome's Capitoline Hill and Palladio's Palazzo Valmarana in Vicenza were approximately contemporary, 1568 and 1565 respectively. Both used a giant order of pilasters as well as secondary and tertiary orders, or layers. Michelangelo's bays were wider, with more visible surface, while Palladio's bays were more

1. Palazzo Nuovo, Rome, Michelangelo

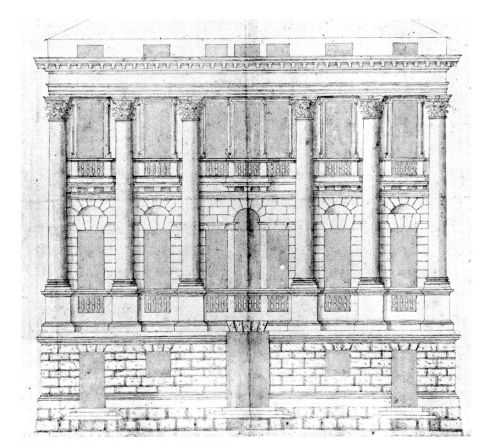

2. Design for a Venetian palace facade, Palladio

3. Palazzo Valmarana Facade, Palladio

4. Palazzo Valmarana secondary order

5. Palazzo Valmarana horizontals

6. Palazzo Valmarana wall

narrow and compressed, which makes the facade appear more transparent. Both bay systems extend evenly across the facade with little central emphasis.

Palladio's remarkable but unbuilt design for a Venetian palace has a very wide central bay with a Serliana window on the piano nobile, analogous to the central bay of the typical Venetian facade.

The giant Corinthian order sits on a rusticated ground floor wall, a flatter version appearing behind the columns on the piano nobile, while the top floor is entirely glazed. Palladio was working in Venice in the sixteenth century, so it would not be surprising to see some reciprocal influence, especially between Palladio and Michele Sanmicheli.

1. Palazzo Zorzi, Mauro Codussi, ca. 1480

2. Palazzo Corner–Spinelli, Mauro Codussi, ca. 1490

Venetian Classicism

Mauro Codussi (1440–1504) was an exceptionally gifted architect from Bergamo, credited with introducing classicism to Venice.

The facade of Codussi's Palazzo Zorzi is among the first uses of white Istrian stone facing for the facade. His Corner–Spinelli follows the three bay Venetian typology, but his side bays replace the blank panel with windows. The facade is planar with very shallow relief.

The ground floor introduces the idea of shallow rustication—which is foreign to the openness of Venice—and the three symmetrical windows on each side of the base exaggerate the discontinuity between the base and the upper two floors. Only the pilasters at the edge of the base extend up to frame and reunite the floors.

The balconies are prominent, but they are horizontally discontinuous, which allows the planar surface of the wall to flow through, firmly establishing the facade as a picture plane, from which the balconies project.

The round arched windows are regularized into a rectangular panel by a small molding, with round medallions punctuating the corners. Other medallions are centered on the panels between windows and align with the capitals to establish a secondary order.

Like earlier Venetian facades, there is no representation of structural loads being carried to the ground (or water).

The Classical Grid

Codussi's Vendramin-Calergi facade is the first use, in Venice, of a classical grid of pilasters, columns, and entablatures to represent structure and order to the wall.[2] The columns are slender, articulate, and spaced apart, so the wall surface appears continuous behind. The heavy horizontals cut the facade into three pieces, but the gridded frame tends to exaggerate the facade's openness. The Palazzo Vendramin–Calergi is an elegant and sophisticated facade—a combination of wall and frame—but, ultimately, the classical grid would predominate in Venice and kill the phenomenal visual characteristics of the traditional Venetian facade.

1. Palazzo Vendramin–Calergi, Mauro Codussi, begun ca. 1502

2. Wall without the classical grid

3. Classical grid without the wall

4. View from the Grand Canal

Scuola Grande di San Marco (Ospedali)

The Scuola Grande di San Marco

Changes in style can be seen within one building, the Scuola Grande di San Marco. The original Scuola on this site burned in 1485. Pietro Lombardo was charged with rebuilding, but in 1490 he was replaced by Mauro Codussi, who finished the building in 1495. Codussi is reputedly credited with the upper part of the facade, including the lunettes and the second floor pediments, but it seems evident that he also was responsible for the window aediculas.

The result is that the facade has two completely different layers, or floors. The ground floor is clearly Lombardo: planar, shallow, refined relief, with minimal classical elements. The upper floor and roof elements are like a different building, more three-dimensional, with heavy classical elements and less apparent wall surface. The grid of pilasters and entablatures helps to somewhat organize and unify the facade, but it still appears to be what it is—a facade designed by two different architects, with two different styles and two different agendas.

The image on the following page is a conjectural fantasy that tries to imagine an approximation of what Lombardo might have done if he had continued with the project: no pediments, more wall surface, and more "freckles" (like cross-sections through round columns).

The most unique elements of the ground floor are the four perspective reliefs by Lombardo's son Tullio. In *The Architectural History of Venice*, Deborah Howard says that these reliefs are "naive rather than impressive" because the perspectives only work from a single point of view. This is not correct, of course.

1. Conjectural reconstruction of the Scuola Grande as if Pietro Lombardo had completed the project rather than Codussi

2. Perspective bay by Tullio Lombardo

3. Ca' Dario, Pietro Lombardo

4. Santa Maria dei Miracoli, Pietro Lombardo

1. Scuola Grande entrance to the *salone* (chapel)

2. Scuola Grande entrance to the *albergo* (meeting room)

3. Scuola Grande entrance

Implied Space

The facade of the Scuola Grande di San Marco is composed of two modified Venetian side bays—widely spaced windows with a blank panel between. The left bay leads to the *salone* (chapel) and the right one leads to the *albergo* (meeting room).

There are two instances of implied space on the ground floor facade, the perspectival reliefs and the steps and entry portal.

Each side bay contains two perspective reliefs, composed together, with a common vanishing point near eye level. Thus, a phenomenal space is implied, like a room, parallel to the plane of the facade and completed transparently behind the entry portals.

Seen frontally, the arches of the main entry appear to recede in perspective depth, even though the actual depth is relatively shallow. With the oblique view, the large, vertical, semi-circular arch and the horizontal semi-circular steps and porch combine to imply an apse-like space in front of the facade. Clearly, the perspectives work from any point of view.

1. Fantasy reconstruction of the implied room on the albergo side

2. Fantasy reconstruction of the implied room on the salone side

Piazza San Marco from the basin

The Piazza San Marco

Jacopo Sansovino (1486–1570) was an accomplished but somewhat boring classical architect. As urban design, however, his work in the Piazza San Marco is superb. Sansovino designed the Mint (begun 1536), the Library of San Marco (begun 1537), and the scheme for the Procuratie Nuove, which were re-aligned to make the Campanile a free-standing element.

The facade of the Library was originally intended to continue around the corner as the facade of the Procuratie Nuove, as Sansovino received this commission before that of the Library. In other words, he originally received an urban design commission rather than an architectural one.

Sansovino died in 1570 and the Procuratie Nuove were continued by Vincenzo Scamozzi, with an additional floor and a smaller cornice. After Scamozzi's death, the wing was completed by Longhena. The shorter western wing (the Napoleonic wing) was demolished in 1807 and rebuilt by Giuseppe Maria Soli between 1808–14.

The urban ribbons of classical architecture in Venice's Piazza San Marco could only have been achieved by an enlightened, centralized authority—especially since they were built incrementally over a long period of time. Not only did these urban ribbons achieve the goal of creating a "modern" Roman Forum, but they also achieved an urban masterpiece and a proper setting for modern *Gran Signori Veneziani*.

The adoption of classicism had already begun in domestic and civil architecture by Lombardo and Codussi.

1. Piazza San Marco

2. Piazza San Marco

1. Elevation view of the Procuratie Vecchie

2. Elevation view of the Procuratie Nuove

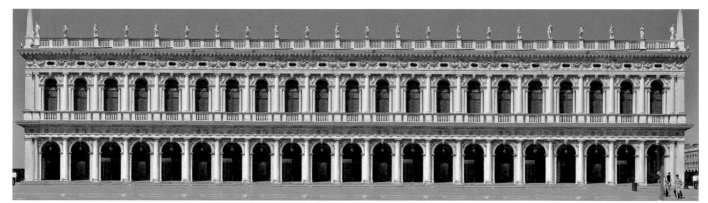

3. Elevation view of the Libreria

4. Elevation view of the Zecca

Comparative Bays of the Procuratie Vecchie, Procuratie Nuove, Libreria, and Zecca at approximately the same scale

The Architecture of the Piazza

It is the repetitive classical bay in white stone that forms the remarkable background—the stage—for the figurative buildings of Venice's Piazza San Marco, the campanile, Doge's Palace, and San Marco.

This idea for making urban walls can be seen as a prelude to the Rue de Rivoli in Paris by Percier and Fontaine and the London terraces by John Nash and George Dance in the early nineteenth century. There are two major differences, however. One is that in Venice the buildings were designed as well as the facades, whereas Nash and Dance designed only the facade bay and the urban plan. The other difference is that Nash and Dance used simpler, planar surfaces—surfaces that made walls—whereas Sansovino designed heavily sculpted bays with little apparent wall. Sansovino's bays are an elaborate concoction of engaged columns, pilasters, entablatures, bas reliefs, etc. The Zecca is the most extreme case. Only Scamozzi's third floor of the Procuratie Nuove has a participating surface. Of all the walls of the Piazza, only the bays of the Procuratie Vecchie, primarily by Bartolomeo Bon, make a planar wall, with the columns in the wall surface.

This classical system of bays was also used for the facades of private houses. Initially, they were adapted to the tripartite Venetian facade system, but soon they spread evenly across the facade to mask the actual bays of the plan. Rusticated ground floors were introduced, and Baroque facades became ever more heavy and elaborate.

1. Palazzo Corner della Ca' Grande, begun after 1545, Sansovino

2. Palazzo Dolfin Manin, begun 1538, Sansovino

Jacopo Sansovino

Sansovino's design of the Palazzo Dolfin Manin is roughly contemporary with his design for the Zecca (the mint), but the buildings could not be more different. The Zecca is a rusticated fortress with even bays. The Palazzo Dolfin Manin also has a classical grid, but no rustication. The classical overlay has relatively shallow relief with much wall surface between the engaged columns. More important, the upper two floors express the traditional three parts of a Venetian palazzo, even though the side bays have a column in the middle of what traditionally would have been a blank panel.

The three bays of the Palazzo della Ca Grande are nearly undetectable on the upper floors and there is no pure wall surface, only high relief.

1. Ca' Rezzonico, begun ca. 1667, Longhena

Baldasari Longhena

Completed more than a century after Codussi's Palazzo Corner-Spinelli, Longhena's Ca' Pesaro has a heavily modeled three-dimensional facade that indicates the typical three bays by double columns. Otherwise, the grid stretches evenly across the facade, as does the rusticated base.

The Ca' Rezzonico has a classical grid across the entire facade, including the rusticated base. There is no discernible wall surface, and the slightly narrower center bays are almost undetectable, thus erasing the most fundamental characteristics of the "Venetian" facade. The plasticity of Longhena's facades is especially foreign to Venice.

2. Ca' Pesaro, Longhena, (completed after 1682 by Antonio Gaspari)

Michele Sanmicheli

Michele Sanmicheli was a much more talented architect than either Sansovino or Longhena, and his facade for the Palazzo Grimani is a genuine masterpiece. It even has hints—memories—of the traditional three bay Venetian facade. Its plasticity—its sculptural depth—and its size make it one of the most complex and aggressive palace facades in Venice.[3]

Like other classical Venetian facades, the Palazzo Grimani has very strong horizontal entablatures dividing the facade into three layers. Two characteristics strongly differentiate it, however: the grid and the sculpted heads above the arches.

The grid, or frame, is not regular. Like Le Corbusier's Villa at Garches, Sanmicheli's facade has a bay rhythm of A:B:A:B:A. But paired columns and pilasters differentiate the two side bays from the three center bays, thus establishing the traditional three-bay typology.

In addition, each of the three floors contains a strongly emphasized mezzanine, which establishes a secondary order that appears to pass transparently behind the primary order of the classical grid of columns, pilasters, and entablatures. This secondary grid has arched windows in the two outer bays and the center bay, and rectangular windows in the two other bays as well as the mezzanine of the lower floor. This, together with paired columns, makes the portego bays read as a Serliana window in the center of the facade.

A third layer of order is formed by the window system on the second and third floors. These windows have substantial horizontals that align with the secondary grid of sub-entablatures to reinforce the reading of this secondary grid. The result of this implicitly continuous grid is the reading of a phenomenal series of overlapping rectangles slipping past the primary grid to transparently unite the three floors.

Finally, the sculpted heads above the arches belong simultaneously to both the entablatures of the primary grid and the arches of the secondary grid. Like the capitals, they punctuate and activate the facade. No other classical facade in Venice is as sophisticated a composition.

1. Palazzo Grimani, wall structure

2. Palazzo Grimani, horizontals

1. Palazzo Grimani, begun 1556, Sanmicheli

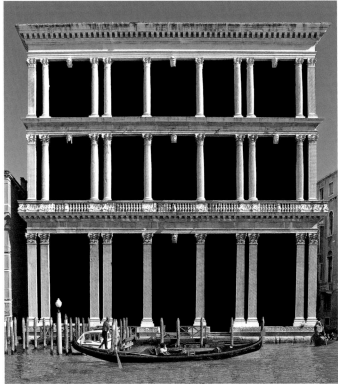

2. Palazzo Grimani, Classical frame without the wall

3. Palazzo Grimani

Casa Pisani Moretta, 15th c.

The Venetian Facade

The Venetian House

The curvilinear canals and streets of Venice promoted deep, narrow-frontage house plans, often in irregular patterns. Most houses had both a water and land entrance, sometimes through a courtyard. The basic plan type consisted of three bays defined by four parallel, structural walls between the water side and the land side. The side bays were divided into ranges of rooms, but the central bay was open through the plan (the *Androne* on the ground floor, the *Portego* on the *Piano Nobile*). Originally, the ground level and mezzanine were for commercial use. Goods were brought in by boat on the water side and stored. Offices were on a mezzanine. The upper level—or levels—were residential, with servants on the attic level.

Various combinations of basic plan and facade types form the building blocks of Venice. Houses were either one, two, or three bays wide and were usually quite deep. The architectural styles changed with the epochs, but the types remained the same for hundreds of years. This is Venice's DNA, providing flexibility, consistency, and endless variety.

The Venetian facade comprises two bay types: a side bay with windows close to the edges and a blank panel between and a central bay of *polifora* openings. Ideally, these bays correspond literally to the bays of the plan. In practice, however, they often do not, as in the Foscari and Giustiniani houses and the Ca' d'Oro, where the facade trumps the plan.

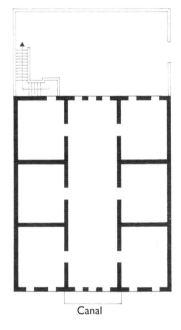

Canal

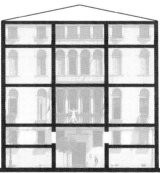

2. Typical Venetian house, plan, and section

1. Typical Venetian house, drawing by Viollet-Le-Duc

3. Typical Venetian house, elevation

Facade Principles

As stated earlier in this study, the term "Venetian" facade refers to the non-classical facades of Venice. The principles of Venetian facades present a sharp contrast to those of classicism and are based on completely different design principles.

Frontality

The concept of "frontality" was introduced in the late nineteenth century by the sculptor Adolf von Hildebrand, who argued that even sculpture in-the-round has a primary, frontal point of view.[1] In architecture, the idea of a facade is intrinsically frontal—a picture plane of shallow, layered space that may also be appreciated from a slightly oblique position.

Transparency

Transparency is the phenomenon created when one incomplete figure appears to be completed by another by apparent overlap. As more figures overlap, visual complexity increases and multiple ambiguous interpretations are possible.[2]

Symmetry and Asymmetry

Classical facades are usually symmetrical, while asymmetrical facades may rely on locally-symmetrical figures and re-centering to establish a more complex order.

Proportion

The classical system utilizes a set of systematic proportional relationships among columns, bays, and facades to develop unified facades. Facades may also utilize similarly proportioned rectangles to achieve unity.

Depth: Literal and Phenomenal

Literal perspective depth, with visible diagonals, is the strongest indication of depth, but phenomenal depth can be suggested by receding figures or by literal diagonals. Literal, non-transparent overlap may also suggest depth.

Vertical and Horizontal Integration

Concepts for interrelating or unifying multi-floor facades include vertical alignment, overlapping surfaces, and uniform grids. The same concepts may also provide horizontal unity.

Figures and Fields

As with faces, figure/field relationships are fundamental to identity and to the composition of architectural facades.

Figures are shapes that require closed contours to be "figural," or identifiable. They may be seen against a neutral "background," or as part of a more complicated gridded field.[3]

The "field" of an architectural facade is comprised of a grid of seen and unseen vertical and horizontal regulating lines. These regulating lines are useful in locating openings, establishing proportional relationships, and relating to the dimensions of the human body. Without figurative interruption, a field of regulating lines might just make a simple, vernacular surface—an "elevation." With more sophisticated design manipulation, however, it might make a facade with one, or multiple, figures.

Small changes in dimension or position can make major changes in the readings of a Venetian facade. The Palazzo Clary, for example, has a simple but elegant tripartite facade. The windows of the side bays are located just far enough from the edges of the bay to make the bays distinct, while establishing continuity of the plane of the facade and emphasizing the figure of the piano nobile portego bay. But if the windows of the side bays are moved slightly closer to the edges of the bays, the figural reading of the facade is completely changed. The planar surface is less continuous, and the portego bay "borrows" the side bay windows for an expanded figure.

1. Palazzo Clary facade

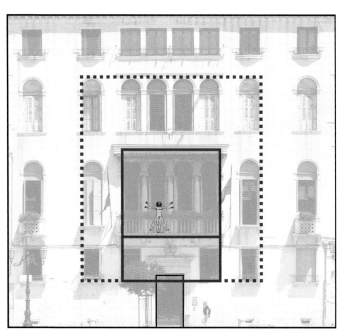

2. Figural readings of the Palazzo Clary facade

3. Adjusted version of the Palazzo Clary facade

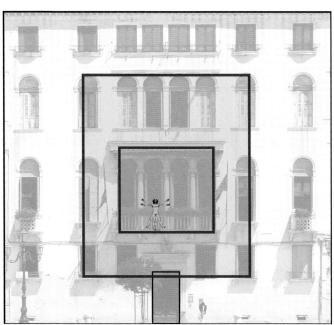

4. Figural readings of the adjusted Palazzo Clary facade

Venetian Facade Types

The classic Venetian house is relatively narrow and deep, with a water entrance in front and a land entrance through a court-yard in back. It is three bays wide: one long, open central bay, with a bay of rooms on either side. Earlier houses were also businesses, and the commercial activities took place on the ground floor. The tall, open hall in the center, the *andron*, was flanked by side bays containing storage rooms with mezzanines, *mesà*, for offices.

The main floor, the piano nobile, was the same except for the mezzanines. The center hall, the *portego*, was open from the water side to the courtyard. There were also other, smaller houses of only one or two bays, and occasionally there were larger buildings with multiple bays.

Venetian facades generally relate to their plans, and are comprised of only two bay types. One, the "side bay," consists of a facade with widely spaced vertical windows with a blank panel between them. The other, the "central bay," consists of a mostly open facade with closely spaced vertical windows, the *curia*.

Single bay houses always have a side bay facade with widely spaced windows and a blank panel between—never (almost never) a central bay facade. Double bay houses may consist of either a symmetrical arrangement of two blank panel side bays, or an asymmetrical arrangement of one side bay and one central bay—never two central bays. Triple bay houses consist of a symmetrical arrangement, one central bay flanked by two side bays. Multiple bay houses are usually achieved by the addition of side bays. Hypothetical examples of each of these types are illustrated below by Photoshop extractions from the Palazzo Clary.

Taken at face value, this system of only two bay types seems rigid and limiting, but just as human beings are all composed of the same basic elements, and yet details and proportions create limitless variety, so too does the Venetian facade system.

1. One side bay

2. Two side bays

3. Two side bays plus an arched window

4. Side bay and center bay

1. Center bay

2. Side bay

3. Two side bays and center bay

4. Three bays plus additional side bays

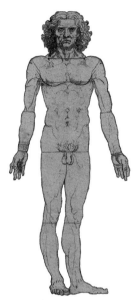

1. Modified Vitruvian man

2. Di Giorgio column 3. Byzantine window

4. Gothic window

5. Renaissance window

Facade Elements and Characteristics

The mesmerizing beauty and unity of Venice is due to two basic factors: the continuous reinterpretation of the same architectural elements and typologies over centuries and the proportional relationships of windows and other elements and their relationships with the human body.

We understand the world through our bodies—our dimensions and our vertical axis. Thus, we cathect with figurative objects, such as columns, and with figurative spaces, such as bays and windows. Windows are especially important as the lenses between the private and public realms. In Venice they are vertical in proportion, and they relate to the dimensions of the human body.

Windows and balconies are the fundamental elements of the Venetian facade. Unelaborated, they would remain as figural "objects" on the surface of the wall, but they are usually extended and elaborated by an entourage of stone panels and moldings. Together with stone bands marking the floors, these moldings form a field of regulating lines framing the figures of the facade.

Before classicism, these moldings were abstract—either rope-shaped for columns, trim, and floor lines, or chain-like moldings called dental moldings (*modenatura a dente*) for edge trim.

When combined vertically on both side bays and center bays, these window compositions emphasize the verticality of both bay types, and therefore the whole facade, rather than the horizontal emphasis of Florentine and Roman facades. Balconies reinforce verticality and further activate the figurative readings of the facade.

All of this contributes to a humanist connection to Venice and its architecture, whether modest or extravagant.

6. Palazzo Barbaro, 13th c.

1. Classical window

2. Rope and dental moldings

3. Palazzo Barbaro side bay

4. Palazzo Barbaro center bay

5. Vertical integration of Gothic windows and balcony

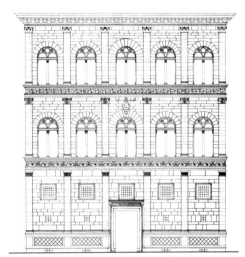

1. Partial elevation of Palazzo Rucellai, Florence

2. Casa Correr, 17th c.

Facade Structure and Order

The load bearing wall was both the representational structure and actual structure of buildings until the modern invention of the columnar frame. The Romans used engaged classical pilasters and columns to represent structure and order the wall. Alberti's reinvention of the system, for the facade of the Palazzo Rucellai in the fifteenth century, became a standard for several hundred years. In Venice, both classical and non-classical representational systems were developed to order facades.

Of the many modest houses on the Grand Canal, the seventeenth-century Casa Correr is perhaps the most modest, even a bit forlorn. Except for the small balcony over the entry, its plaster facade is devoid of architectural detail—an abstract diagram of a Venetian house type— the windows reading as inactive figurative voids on a neutral surface. Cleaned up, without the balcony and arches, and with exposed brick, the building could easily be imagined as contemporary Dutch social housing, or the product of any number of rationalist contemporary architects.

The following images from various epochs illustrate digitally altered Venetian facades superimposed on that of the Casa Correr to demonstrate various ways of charging and activating the Casa Correr facade.[4] Just as windows had been given entourage to subdue and meld them into the surface of the wall, architects expanded the technique to the whole facade, thereby integrating figure and field, while simultaneously creating multiple figural readings and overlapping fields.

Materials were important. Typically, the rough brick walls of Venetian houses were covered with colored or painted plaster for a smooth, pale surface. Window trim and other architectural details such as balconies and cornices were made of hard, white Istrian stone.

Classical facades were faced entirely with stone, however, and were modeled with great depth—plasticity. This, together with the classical grid, ultimately killed the vitality of the traditional Venetian facade.

1. Casa Correr with modified Ca' Foscari

2. Casa Correr with modified 16th Century residence

3. Casa Correr with modified Giustinian Michiel Alvise

4. Casa Correr with modified Ca' Grande

1. Fondaco dei Turchi, 13th c. (19th c. renovation)

2. Fondaco dei Turchi, 13th c.

3. Villa Trissino at Cricoli

Early Venetian Houses

The earliest surviving houses in Venice include the Fondaco dei Turchi (previously owned by the Pesaro family and questionably renovated in the nineteenth century), the Ca' Loredan, Ca' Farsetti, and the Ca' da Mosto. These Byzantine period houses were built during the thirteenth century and all give some indication of the beginnings of the Venetian facade system.

All four houses have arcades in the central sections on the ground floor and piano nobile—an obvious source for the central bays of later houses. All four also have indications of differentiated side bays, but they are very subtly articulated. These tower-like corner elements, or *torresselle*, had mainland precedents in the Roman villas such as the Villa Trissino at Cricoli —a villa significantly renovated by Giangiorgio Trissino in the sixteenth century—but they do not have widely spaced windows separated by a blank panel. Thus, one of the two bays of the prototypical Venetian facade is of unclear origin.

Some say that the purpose of the widely spaced windows is to let in light along the perpendicular walls. Others say the purpose is to provide a place for a fireplace behind the blank part of the wall, though in practice this is often not the case. Whatever the reason, the blank panel bay is a crucial component of Venetian facades.

1. Ca' Loredan and Ca' Farsetti, 13th c.

2. Conjectural reconstruction of Ca' da Mosto, 13th c.   3. Ca' da Mosto, with additional floors

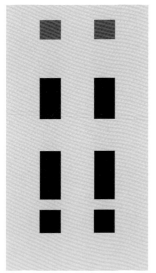

1. Normal row house facade diagram

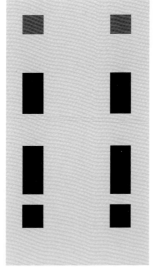

2. Venetian single bay facade diagram

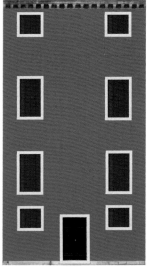

3. Windows with trim only

The Single Bay Facade

There are many single bay houses in Venice. Almost none of them are the type or format of the center bay of the typical three-part Venetian house. Rather, they are the peculiar outer, or side bay type. They are essentially row houses and could just as easily have had evenly spaced windows. Instead, for unclear reasons, they have widely spaced windows with a blank wall between.

Tall, narrow facades with windows widely spaced near the outer edges of the wall may seem like a boring facade diagram, but it is the ancillary elements that enliven the basic diagram and push it into a virtually unlimited range of variations.

The basic wall of the Venetian house is made of rough brick masonry requiring stone trim for all openings. It also requires a finished surface, usually plaster or stone veneer.

Balconies are not common in Florence or Rome, but they play a major role in Venetian facades. They extend the verticality of windows, they can be horizontally continuous or discontinuous, and they may vary from floor to floor—all of which promote an infinite variety of figural readings. Balconies also add a dramatic scenographic characteristic of public display.

The ancillary elements, all in white Istrian stone, include simple window trim, balconies, small cornices, edge trim and quoining, window and door eyelids, and horizontal bands and tracery.

These elements enable the windows, balconies, etc. to be combined to form larger, figural groupings, which may be further related, to form even larger figures. For example, the tops of mezzanine windows are often pushed up to touch the balconies of the piano nobile, and the windows of the piano nobile are stretched to touch the balconies above them to make virtually continuous vertical stripes. The horizontal, white stone tracery renders visible the gridded field of the facade and locks in the figural elements.

It is the almost mystic quality of the blank panel that makes these single bay facades so fascinating, and the addition of a single emblem in the middle of the panel can activate it. When these elements are combined into double bay facades, the possibilities of this facade type expand geometrically.

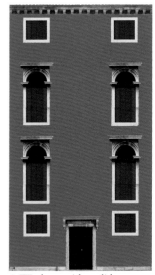

4. Windows with eyelids

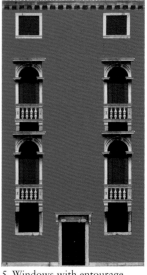

5. Windows with entourage

House in the Campo dei Frari

1. Palazzo Barbarigo della Terrazza

2. Casa Volpi, 17th–18th c.

3. Casa Luccatello, 17th c.

4. Hotel Regina, 19th c.

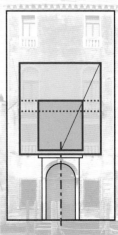

1. Palazzo Da Mula, 15th c.

2. Palazzo Da Mula facade studies

Palazzo Pisani, 17th c.

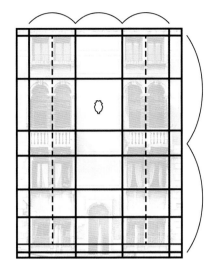
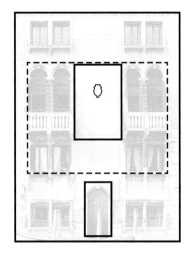

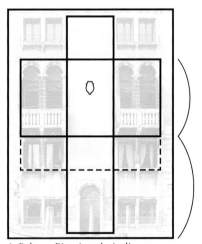
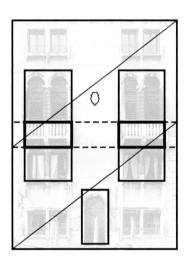

1. Palazzo Pisani analysis diagrams

The Palazzo Pisani

The facade of the Palazzo Pisani is perhaps the most complex and interesting of all the side bay facades. The double arched windows, with windows immediately below the balconies, the stone quoins and tracery, and the compressed central panel all contribute to a multiplicity of possible overlapping readings of this simple facade. The water level windows are very low on the facade and make it seem like the building is sinking, were it not for the watergate itself, which is identical in size and surround to the arched windows above.

2. Palazzo Pisani

3. Palazzo Pisani variations

Palazzo Contarini-Fasan, late-15th c.

Composite Single Bay Houses

There are very few single center bay houses in Venice, but there are some interesting composite single bays—usually, a side bay over a center bay. One beautiful example is the fifteenth-century Gothic Palazzo Contarini-Fasan. Rather than a two story asymmetrical house, the solution was to put the side bay on top of the center bay. The ground floor (with no direct entry) is of sufficient height relative to the upper floors as not to seem awkward.

Two adjoining single bay houses on the Cannaregio Canal are similar to the Palazzo Contarini-Fasan in type but with very compressed ground floors, which makes them appear to be sinking. The house on the right is a disguised side bay type. The white framework and balcony on the piano nobile obscure the blank panel and combine with the white stone of the ground floor. This benefits from the vertical alignment of the door and upper panels, integrating the door into the overall composition, which ameliorates the proportions of the compressed ground floor.

Houses on the Fondamenta Cannaregio

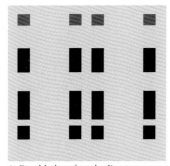

1. Double bay facade diagram

2. Palazzo Loredan Cini, 16th c.

3. Palazzo Fornoni, 16th c.

4. Palazzo Barbaro, local centers

5. Palazzo Emo, 18th c.

6. Palazzo, 17th c.

The Double Side Bay House

The idea of putting two side bay facades together to make a double-bay house seem unpromising. It is a revelation, however, that such a low-grade idea actually produces much complexity and variety. In fact, the Palazzo Barbaro facade rivals the best in Venice. Balconies, both continuous and discontinuous, are primary contributors to the compositional possibilities.

It doesn't take much, as small details such as the difference between joined or separate balconies can transform the appearance of the facade. For example, the central balconies on the first piano nobile of the Palazzo Barbaro are close, but are separate. On the second piano nobile they are joined and the windows have white stone surrounds, making a figure within a figure.

Palazzo Barbaro

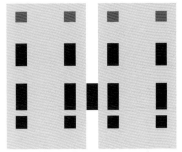

1. Double-Single Bay + House diagram

The Double Side Bay House +

The idea of a double bay house with a thin "spacer" between them—an extra window—yields a surprising array of compositional possibilities. Because the interior windows of the side bays link-up with the center "spacer" window, most of these facades read as a center, or portego, bay with outlying windows near the edges of the facade.

The use of a gridded white stone strapping, or tracery, tends to stretch the facade to the edges like a taut membrane, while elevating the blank panels to more active participation with the composition.

Details and proportion are important. More space between windows, or between the outer windows and the edges of a facade, make a major difference in the reading of the facade. For example, the sixteenth-century facade below is more static. There is no stone grid, so the windows read simply as objects on a surface which extends continuously from edge to edge. In contrast, the facade of the Palazzo Giustinian Michiel Alvise has a contrasting grid that extends to the edges, but with wall surface and no quoining. This activates the surface with multiple overlapping readings and emphasizes the edges as well.

2. Palazzo, 16th c.

3. Palazzo, 19th c.

4. Palazzo Giustinian Michiel Alvise, 17th c.

5. Palazzo Mangilli Valmarana, 18th c.

6. Palazzo Civran, 18th c.

7. Palazzo Miani Coletti Giusti, 18th c.

74

1. Palazzo

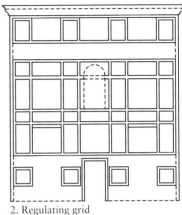

2. Regulating grid

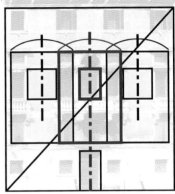

3. Overlapping fields and figures

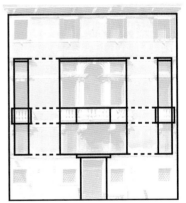

4. Figures

When the outer windows of the side bays are located flat against the party walls on each side and when there is a field of contrasting white stone bands connecting the architectural elements, the facade appears to have been stretched tight horizontally. Counterintuitively, this also has the effect of compressing the blank panels and putting them in competition with the three-dimensional architectural elements. Further, when the inner windows of the side bays touch the frame of the central "spacer" window, the space is absorbed into a dominant figure, like a portego bay. This creates three overlapping fields: the two rectangles of the side bays and the composite rectangle of the "phenomenal" portego bay.

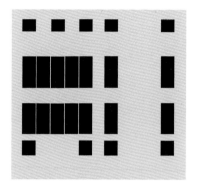

1. Asymmetric Double-Bay house diagram

2. Palazzo Duodo, 15th c.

3. Palazzo Molin Erizzo, 15th c.

Side and Center Bay Houses

Composed of one side bay and one portego bay, this house type is not the most prevalent in Venice, but it may be the most interesting due to its asymmetry.

Early Gothic facades, such as the Palazzo Duodo, were simple, planar surfaces with figural windows floating on the surface, ordered only by their alignment. Gradually, these figures became more organized into a field by panelized window tracery, floor-line string courses, and substantive, white stone balconies.

A persistent visual problem with the Venetian facade was that the ground floor was often quite low. This tended to make the entry door appear too squat for the building and also make the building appear to be sinking. This was addressed by extending the apparent height of the entry and absorbing it into a larger figure, as in the Palazzo Morosini-Sagredo—or both, as in the Palazzo Badoer-Tiepolo.

In the sixteenth century, the planar surface of the facade became increasingly organized as a field by more developed stone tracery, forming a grid of regulating lines. This more developed grid promoted the expansion of overlapping figures, as in the facade of the Palazzo Barbarigo. It also

4. Palazzo Morosini-Sagredo, 14th c.

turned the blank panels of the side bay into active figural participants in the composition of the facade. The combination of equal windows and extended grid tended to stretch the facade into a taut membrane.

These were well-behaved facades that were at once individual, artistic achievements and part of the continuous urban

1. Palazzo Barbarigo, 16th c.

2. Palazzo Badoer Tiepolo, 17th c.

3. House on the Grand Canal with local centers, 16th c.

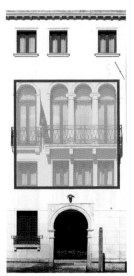

4. Local symmetries

fabric of the city. Oddly, the sixteenth-century house on the right has no literal grid, only an abstract (almost modern) planar surface, but is a sophisticated urban facade with very complex overlapping figural readings and multiple local symmetries. The overall reading is asymmetrical, but the center axis of the facade stabilizes it.

Palazzo Donà in Campo S. M. Formosa

1. Campo S. M. Formosa

The Palazzo Donà

Most of the campi in Venice are formed by low-key, unpretentious buildings. The Campo Santa Maria Formosa has more high quality facades than most Venetian campi, however. In fact, the northwest side of the campo is defined by a series of interesting Gothic facades. At first glance, the Palazzo Donà, located in the middle, blends unselfconsiously into the line of cacophonous facades, appearing to be a standard combination of side bay and portego bay. A closer look reveals a more complex, oddly agitated facade with shifting symmetries and overlapping readings.

Most noticeably, the facade has no horizontal or vertical continuity. It is as if each floor was planned independently of the others, with the piano nobile being the most egregiously different floor. Nevertheless, these idiosyncrasies produce the quirky, interesting compositional freedom of the facade.

2. Portego bay

3. Side bay

1. Full six-light window panel, including balconies framed by pilasters

4. Conjectural facade with the piano nobile removed

2. Five-light portego bay

5. Top floor

6. Piano nobile

7. First floor

8. Ground floor

3. Four-light window panel with three round columns between pilasters

1. Palazzo Donà in Campo S. M. Formosa

2. Entry door

The ground floors of the Palazzo Donà and adjacent buildings are all disproportionately low, relative to the upper floors and heights of the buildings. The height of the actual entry door of the Palazzo Donà, however, is visually extended vertically by the Gothic arch above it. This forms a composite figure with the two Gothic windows touching the arch, and despite a bit of misalignment, this influence extends vertically to absorb the entire side bay.

It should also be noted that the idiosyncrasies of the Palazzo Donà facade are complimented and extended by the facades of the adjacent buildings.

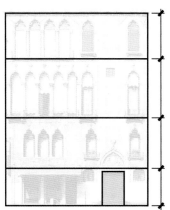

3. Diagram of relative floor heights

The Ca' Dario

Many of the most beautiful Venetian houses are two bays wide: one side bay and one central bay, thereby making the facade asymmetrical. The portego bay with three arched windows is sometimes narrower than the side bay with the blank panel, but the proximity of the side bay windows makes a larger figure, and therefore, it seems like the portego bay is wider.

In these facades, there are four local symmetries. One is the symmetry around the vertical axis of the side bay, which is framed by two narrow, white pilasters. The second is the symmetry around the vertical axis of the portego bay, which has two round columns in the center and is framed by two narrow, white pilasters. The third is the symmetry around the vertical axis of the composite figure of the portego bay plus the adjacent side bay window. Finally, there is the symmetry of the overall facade.

The Ca' Dario facade is the most elaborate version of this type. Its primary reading is asymmetrical due to the four arched windows on the left side, but the center of the facade is established by the symmetry of the ground floor entry and windows and by the windows of the side bay.

This facade is also unique due to the proliferation of round elements on the surface. Like cross sections of columns, they enliven and give a plan-like quality to the facade.

Ca' Dario, 1480s

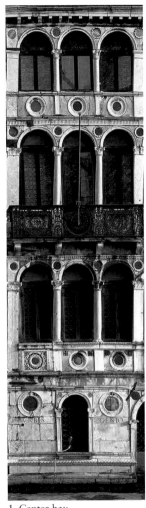

1. Center bay

2. Side bay

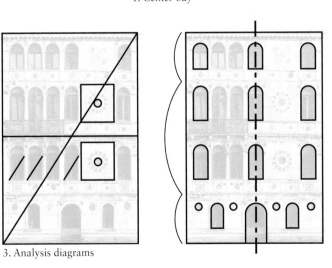

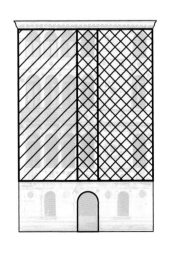

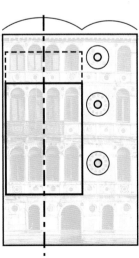

3. Analysis diagrams

Ca' d'Oro facade

The Ca' d'Oro

Built on the Grand Canal between 1421 and 1443 for the merchant Marino Contarini, the Ca' d'Oro has a facade that has been described by Deborah Howard in *The Architectural History of Venice* as "incoherent." While it is true that there are many oddities and inconsistencies about the facade, it is one of the most beautiful and complex Venetian facades. Its original appearance was apparently garish, with many brightly painted and gilded surfaces, but its simpler contemporary state is remarkable for its plethora of ideas. This does not mean that these ideas were intentional by the authors, as they certainly were not. Historians must deal with factual and chronological correctness, but architects deal with ideas—design ideas. This means that "historic artifacts" can provide fresh ideas and interpretations for contemporary design in spite of their original intent.

Like the Ca' Dario, the Ca' d'Oro is a two-bay facade composed of one central bay and one side bay. It is primarily asymmetrical, relatively flat, with no classical elements. The interaction between the gridded field of the facade and the multiple figural readings is one of the most complex in Venice.

Like almost all classical facades, the facade of the Ca' d'Oro is a load bearing wall. Unlike classical facades, however, the facade of the Ca' d'Oro has no representation of loads being carried to the ground (or water). In fact, not even the structural columns on the three floors align with the columns below, thus contributing to the taught, membrane-like quality of the facade. Rather, the Ca' d'Oro facade is like a tapestry hung from the cornice—a picture plane, punctured by deep spatial openings and projecting balconies. In this sense, it can be considered an ancestor, or a descendant, of Le Corbusier's Villa at Garches.

Although there are no classical elements on the Ca' d'Oro facade, it exploits an elaborately developed set of artistic principles: figure/field relationships, symmetry/asymmetry, local symmetry/re-centering, unifying proportional relationships, literal/phenomenal depth, transparency, and multiple readings. Finally, the white Istrian stone and colored marble of the facade combine to form a continuous, pale pastel surface that changes according to different light and water conditions.[5]

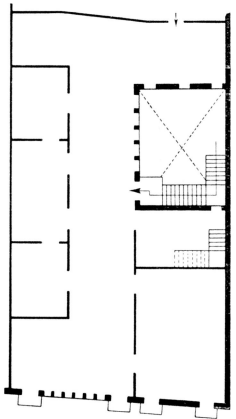

Ca' d'Oro, piano nobile plan

Facade and Plan

Normally, there is a direct relationship between a Venetian facade and the plan behind it, but sometimes the facade trumps the plan with a life of its own. In this case, like the Palazzi Giustiniani and Ca' Foscari, the Ca' d'Oro facade takes precedence over its plan. The Ca' d'Oro has an asymmetrical two-bay facade, but only the side bay coincides literally with the large bay of the plan; the portego bay spans two narrower plan bays. The plan is perfunctory; clearly, the facade is intended as a major public presentation along the Grand Canal.

1. Ca' d'Oro facade

2. Fantasy collage of an alternative Ca' d'Oro facade

The Two Bay Facade

At first glance, one of the most striking things about the facade of the Ca' d'Oro is the pronounced difference between the two bays. The portego bay is almost completely porous, while the side bay is a mostly opaque surface. In addition, due to phenomenal overlap, both bays appear to be close to the same size. Thus, they almost read like separate buildings with a decorative vertical strip between them. This may be at least partially the result of the width of the site, which was determined by the Palazzo Zen, which was demolished to build the Ca' d'Oro.

A narrower site might have produced a more normative but less interesting design, such as the fantasy alternative above. With the actual facade, it is the windows, balconies, and floor lines that stretch across the whole facade and help unify it.

Details are important. Three windows on the piano nobile—the central one (with "Leo") and the two outer ones—are unique, and their balconies are wider. They stretch across the entire facade and establish an overall symmetry about the central window. On the top floor, four smaller identical windows with smaller balconies also extend across the entire facade, reinforcing the piano nobile windows below.

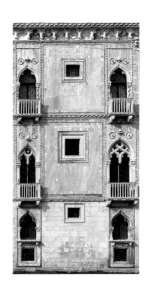

3. Portego bay, connection panel, and side bay

1. Doge's Palace, second floor loggia detail

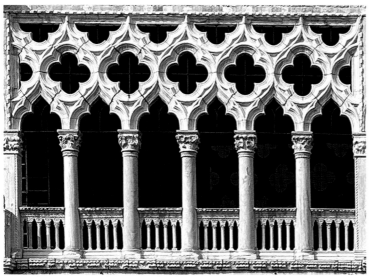

2. Ca' d'Oro, piano nobile loggia detail

Primary Figures

Multiple overlapping figures vie for dominance in the Ca' d'Oro facade. For example, initially, the six-light portego screen of the piano nobile appears to be the dominant figure of the Ca' d'Oro facade. But then the larger rectangle of both portego screens appears stronger. Then the loggia openings on the lower level expand that reading, followed by the adjacent windows.

The six-light portego opening is derived from the facade of the Doge's Palace (1341–1424). The Ca' d'Oro was finished in 1428. This unique structural system is more like an elaborate screen than an expression of structural loads being carried to the ground. This is exacerbated by the clipping of the column tops on each side and by the lack of structural alignment of the columns from one floor to the next. This screen absorbs the dark depth of the space behind, making it appear flat, as part of the screen.

3. Primary figures

The Field

The regulating lines of the Ca' d'Oro facade are formed by abstracted stone ropes and dental moldings. These nautically derived forms establish the facade edges, the floor lines, and the window panel borders. Stone ropes and dental moldings even encircle the round medallions in the window panels and the arches of the windows and loggias. These regulating lines define vertical and horizontal zones or bands, which, in turn, form the fabric of the facade.

Windows

The Ca' d'Oro window openings and their immediate surrounds would read as objects (figures) on the facade, but this potential reading is ameliorated by the enhancements of the basic windows by moldings, panels, medallions, and balconies that expand their influence.

Dental moldings surround the windows and extend to the floor lines above, with round medallions defined by rope moldings in the panel above the actual window and sculptural caps to the pointed arches.

These panels serve to bring the window openings into active participation with the surface of the facade.

The corded window panels stretch the effect of the windows from floor to floor to contribute to the grid of the facade. The windows and panels on the top floor are all equal, but on the piano nobile three windows are different, reinforcing the symmetry of the facade. The ground floor windows of the side bay do not even touch the bottom of the facade, thus emphasizing this tapestry-like quality. And, in a final paradox, the six-light window panels on the left appear flat, whereas the panels of the side bay suggest perspectival depth by nested rectangles.

Balconies

Balconies are not common active elements of Renaissance palaces, but in Venice they play a primary role. They mediate between the private interior and the civic pageantry of the exterior by providing a point of display and retreat. Formally, bal-

1. Piano nobile window, side bay

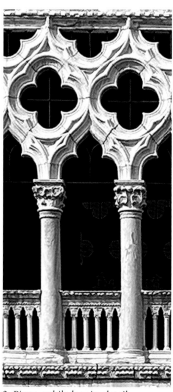

2. Piano nobile loggia, detail

3. Piano nobile window, portego

4. Piano nobile window, side bay

5. Second piano nobile window

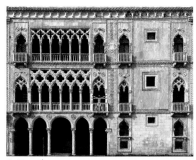

1. Facade

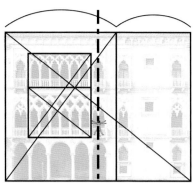

2. Proportional diagram

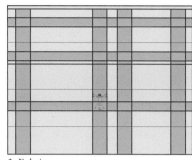

3. Fabric

conies are also one of the most important elements in the composition of the Venetian facade. By projecting from the picture plane they simultaneously activate the facade and reinforce its fabric.

Almost all balconies in Venice are substantive Istrian stone elements. Transparent balconies of metal, such as those of the Ca' Dario, are rare. The balconies of the Ca' d'Oro consist of a thick floor slab supported by projecting brackets, square corner posts, and a thick top "rail" supported by closely spaced, thin columns with abstracted capitals.

While most Venetian balconies project from the plane of the facade, the balcony of the six-light screen of portego columns of the Ca' d'Oro are an exception. Here, the balcony is attached to the rear of the columns and appears to pass behind the columns. This allows the screen of columns to be read from floor to floor as a complete figure, uninterrupted by balconies. The primary figure of the facade is thus absorbed into the grid of the facade while exaggerating the importance of the other balconies.

The window panels are pushed up tight below the balconies, creating a continuous vertical zone that links to the horizontal zones of the facade. These vertical zones of windows and balconies seem to hang from the cornice, and on the side bay they do not touch the water, thus adding to the sense of weightlessness.

Despite their flatness, the blank panels on the upper two floors demonstrate the phenomenon of perspective depth due to a series of nested rectangles that appear to recede from the picture plane. On the lower level, a similar perspectival phenomena occurs due to the three square-ish windows.

Proportions

Proportional relationships reinforce both the fabric and the figures of the facade. The whole facade, the portego bay, the portego screen on the upper two floors, and the portego screen on the piano nobile all have the same proportion.

4. Side bay, detail

1. Ca' d'Oro facade

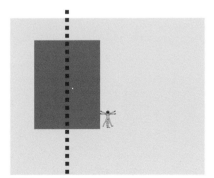

2. Primary figure

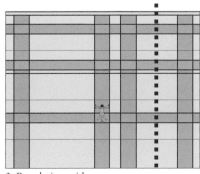

3. Regulating grid

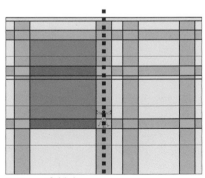

4. Figure/field diagram

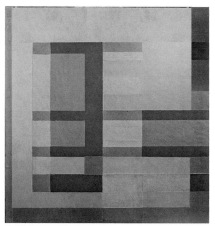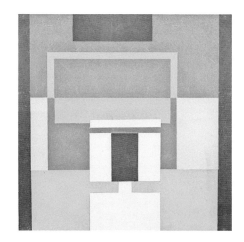

1. Color studies

Asymmetry and Re-centering

The principle of re-centering relies on locally symmetrical figures. The facade of the Ca' d'Oro has three local symmetries. One is the portego bay; the second is that of the side bay; the third is that of the whole facade, the axis of which is marked by "Leo" in the picture. The facade also has a complex interaction between the gridded field and multiple figural readings.

Figure/Field Relationships

The concept, or phenomenon, of figure/field—sometimes referred to as figure/ground—in architecture and urban design is usually associated with urban plans, where built solids are black, or grey, and civic space is white. Either might be figurative, but with the traditional city, the urban fabric is usually the "ground." This idea may have some value in urban design, but it is not useful in a discussion of facade design.

The concept of figure/field is more useful when the two are integrated as fabric.

The eye and mind are capable of absorbing and understanding complex visual relationships at once, without explanation and without historical reference. This, and the concept of transparency, enable complex figure/field relationships.

Figurative elements are identified by perimeter closure. They may appear to exist against a neutral background as a simple relationship with an unambiguous reading, but when there is a reciprocal relationship between figure and field—when figures are embedded—the two elements form a fabric where possible readings can multiply geometrically. Just as the mind becomes convinced of one reading or interpretation, another reading emerges as equally plausible. One can alternatively imagine that the fabric of the field is manipulated to provoke images to emerge, or, alternatively, that images are absorbed into the field by "stitching" them into the fabric. Either way a reciprocal relationship is developed between figure and field, resulting in the *fabric* of the facade.[6]

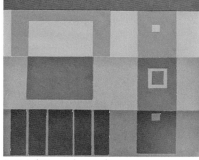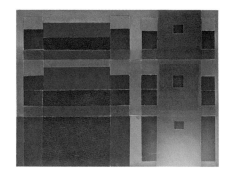

2. Ca' d'Oro color studies

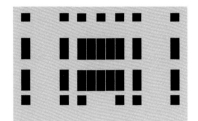

1. Three bay facade diagram

2. Ca' Foscari, begun ca. 1450

3. Ca' Rezzonico, begun 1667

Three Bay Facades

The issues previously discussed are compounded and multiplied with three bay facades, and new characteristics emerge.

As the facades become wider, they approach square, or near-square proportions, which accentuates the tapestry-like quality of the non-classical Venetian facade. In contrast to classical Venetian facades, such as Ca' Rezzonico, whose evenly-spaced columns create a static reading with literal depth, the non-classical facades emphasize the plane of the vertical surface and give no indication of weight, or weight being carried down. The facade of the Ca' Corner Mocenigo by Sanmicheli (after 1537) even has a separation between the stone-trimmed upper stories and the rusticated base of the ground floor. In other words, no vertical elements from the top continue to the base; the top simply floats above the rustication. These facades seem more at home on the water, as well as on the *fondamente*, than classical facades like the Ca' Rezzonico.

The central figures of these three bay facades are also bigger, as they can visually expand laterally. When there are two main floors they can also visually expand vertically.

Another important characteristic, especially of later three bay facades, is the increased role of lattices of flat, white Istrian stone bands that delineate the grid, or fabric, of the facade. These bands facilitate the possibility of visually overlapping rectangles and unify the facade by stretching it taut to the outside edges. It also allows the glass to appear as a continuous plane behind the surface.

It is surprising how much glass there is in these facades and how little actual wall surface is needed to establish the plane of the facade.

1. Palazzo Michiel dalle Colonne, 17th c.

2. Palazzo Castelli

3. Palazzo Grimani Marcello, 16th c.

4. Palazzo Mocenigo

5. Palazzo Contarini Cavalli, 15th c.

6. Palazzo Michiel della Brusa, 15th c.

Palazzo Brandolin-Rota, 17th c.

The Palazzo Brandolin-Rota

This seventeenth-century palazzo is located on the Grand Canal between the Accademia and the sixteenth-century Palazzo Contarini dal Zaffo. It is typologically similar to the Contarini dal Zaffo, as well as the sixteenth-century Palazzo Grimani Marcello, but, in comparison, it is far more complex and interesting than either of these Venetian Renaissance facades. There are several reasons for this.

First, the Brandolin-Rota facade has few classical elements except the balconies and watergate; the facade is purely planar, without pilasters, entablatures, or round medallions. Second, the windows of the side bays are close to the outer edges of the bays, which proportionally emphasizes the blank panel between them and allows the inner windows to read together with those of the portego bay, thus expanding its figural reading. Third, the white stone tracery forms a regulating grid that unifies the facade and its elements into a fabric of multiple figures and a stabilizing field. Finally, the balconies on the piano nobile simultaneously establish the identity of the three individual bays, the taut lateral extent of the facade, and the expanded figure of the central bay. The upper balcony collaborates with the balcony separations below to reaffirm the authority of the portego bay and the watergate zone.

It is interesting that there appears to be complete continuity of surface, but 44% of the facade is open. In contrast, the facade of the Villa Garches is only 35% open.

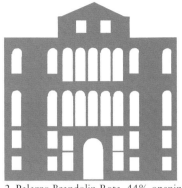

2. Palazzo Brandolin-Rota, 44% opening

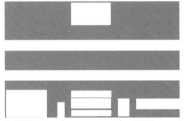

3. Villa Garches, same scale, 35% opening

1. Palazzo Brandolin-Rota, center bay

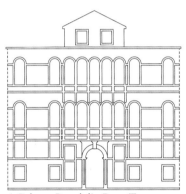

4. Palazzo Brandolin-Rota, Tracery

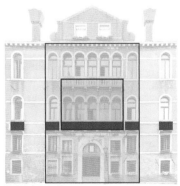

5. Multiple figures

6. Original facade, conjectural reconstruction

95

1. Palazzo Mocenigo, Casa Nuova   Palazzetto Mocenigo   Palazzetto Mocenigo   Palazzo Mocenigo, Casa Vecchia

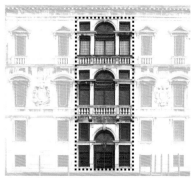

2. Casa Nuova, central figures

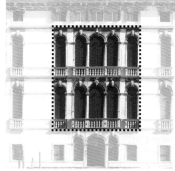

3. Casa Vecchia, central figures

4. Palazzo Mocenigo, Casa Nuova

5. Palazzo Mocenigo, Casa Vecchia

1. Casa Nuova, center bay

2. Casa Vecchia, center bay

Palazzi Mocenigo

There are four contiguous Mocenigo palaces along the Grand Canal. The first, the Casa Vecchia, was originally a Gothic house. The second, the Casa Nuova, was finished around 1579. The two middle *palazzetti* were the last to be built, in the second half of the sixteenth century. All four facades have a similar tripartite parti, but the Casa Nuova is the most overtly classical and this makes a notable contrast with the Casa Vecchia.

The older palace is simpler, with more overlapping figures, and is more unified. Both facades have a regulating grid of tracery, but the Casa Nuova has a higher degree of plasticity due to panels, pediments, emblems, etc. It also has a greater variety of openings, and the balcony on the first piano nobile is limited to the central bay, whereas the balconies on the second piano nobile span the entire facade. This and the window pediments contribute to a sharp distinction between the two side bays and the center portego bay. The facade of the Casa Vecchia is the opposite. The surface is more planar, with similar window openings; balconies on both floors span the whole facade; and the bays are more similar.

The space between the side and center bays is crucial to the readings of a facade. It is similar in width on both the Casa Vecchia and Casa Nuova, but the characteristics cited above allow the narrow portego bay of the Casa Vecchia to "borrow" windows from the side bays to increase the figural emphasis of the center.

1. Palazzo Corner Mocenigo, Michele Sanmicheli, 1551–64

1. Structural wall

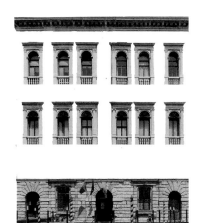
2. Classical elements

3. Classical elements with strapping

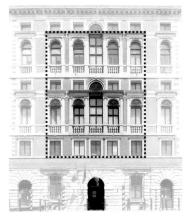
4. Primary figures

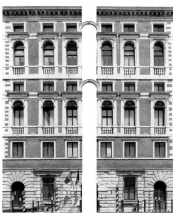
5. Two part system

6. Discontinuity between base and top

Michele Sanmicheli II

The facade of the Palazzo Corner Mocenigo is Sanmicheli's most enigmatic work. Like most classical Venetian facades, the building emphasizes lateral continuity and evenness that tends to suppress the three-part Venetian system. Vertically there is a shocking contrast and discontinuity between the rusticated base, reminiscent of Sanmicheli's fortified gates in Verona and the relatively flat refinement of the upper stories. Unlike Sanmicheli's Palazzo Grimani, there is no superimposed grid of classical columns and entablatures. In fact, other than the base and cornice, the only overt classical elements are the aediculas framing the windows; everything else is abstract strapping in low-relief, white Istrian stone set against burnt sienna colored plaster. Normally, one would expect the base and upper part of the facade to be joined, but there is a gap between them with no stone connection—no quoining, no pilasters or columns, no strapping. As a result, the upper stories appear to be suspended from the cornice with no connection to the ground, merely hovering above the rusticated base. The white lattice of the upper stories also gives the impression of a significant proportion of openness and transparency to the wall, but the drawing of the load-bearing wall and window penetrations is surprisingly dense, without a significant proportion of openings. It is the white tracery that extends the influence of the windows, making the facade appear more open. Because of the horizontal continuity of this tracery, and because the side and center bays are equal in width, the three-part system is subdued, and the height of the central windows makes the facade appear as a two-part system linked by arches. Finally, the figurative aspects of the facade are also subdued, but visible.

7. Hypothetical integration of base and top

Palazzo Maffetti-Tiepolo, 17th c.

1. Portego bay

2. Side bay

3. Side bay

The Palazzo Maffetti-Tiepolo

This seventeenth-century palazzo by Domenico Rossi, along with the Gothic Palazzi Soranzo, form part of the long, curved, eastern enclosure of the Campo S. Polo. With superb facades, these palazzi originally faced a canal, which was filled in 1761. The surface of the white stone facade of the Palazzo Maffetti-Tiepolo has very shallow relief, but closely-spaced windows and semi-continuous balconies tend to even out the three parts of the facade. Despite an opening to surface ratio of 32% to 68%, the facade appears to be open and frame-like. Indeed, the entire center section reads as an open frame. The blank side panels are the only real indication of surface.

4. View from the campo

5. Structural wall

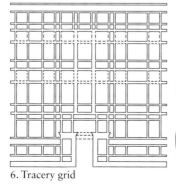

6. Tracery grid

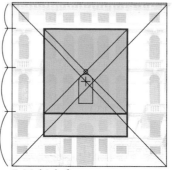

7. Multiple figures.

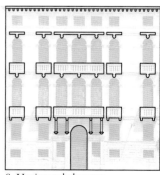

8. Horizontal elements

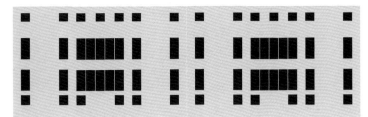

1. Double house facade diagram

2. Double palazzo in Campo San Stin

Double Facades

One means of growth is to mirror image one house into two identical ones, such as the Palazzo Bembo and the two Mocenigo palazzi below. A more picturesque and interesting version is not a symmetrical mirror image, but an asymmetrical doubling, as seen with Palazzo Soranzo and the Palazzo Giustinian on the following pages.

When bays or buildings are repeated, curious readings may appear. Things that are minor in one composition can take on major importance with repetition. For example, there are three large, square windows on the ground floor of the Palazzo Soranzo. The one in the center is nominally central to the whole building, but the whole building is not symmetrical.

3. Palazzo Bembo, 15th c.

4. Two of the four contiguous Palazzi Mocenigo on the Grand Canal

1. Palazzo of the Ghetto Nuovissimo on the rio degli Ormesini, 16th c.

2. Palazzi Soranzo, begun mid-14th c.

1. Palazzi Giustiniani, begun shortly before 1451

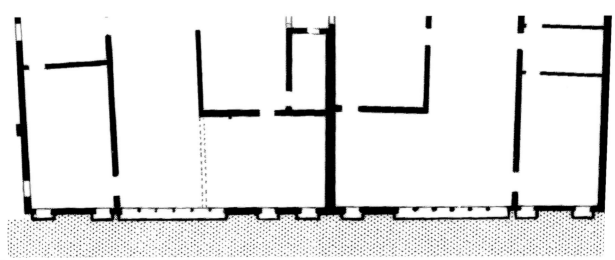

2. Palazzi Giustiniani, plan of second piano nobile

The Palazzi Giustiniani

At first glance, the facades of these two palaces along the Grand Canal appear to be one large, symmetrical, and unified facade, with a central watergate and canal articulating the two palaces. Initially, each palace appears to be a traditional, symmetrical, tripartite Venetian type with a central watergate—as in the regularized image below.

This reading escapes quickly upon further study, however, as the facade is in fact highly agitated, with multiple local symmetries. It then appears to consist of two asymmetrical, bipartite Venetian types—each similar to the Ca' d'Oro—joined by a third central, symmetrical facade.

The appearance of asymmetry is precipitated solely by the second piano nobile, as the "ground" floor, second floor (first piano nobile), and top floors are completely symmetrical. The second piano nobile has six-lite openings to the portego instead of four as on the first piano nobile. Were it not for this floor's unique windows flanking the facade's center, the reading would be two tripartite facades with overlapping side bays.

All of this complexity and agitation is produced by the lack of congruence between plan and facade on the second piano nobile, emphasizing the autonomy and importance of the Venetian facade. This facade is no accident, but intentional—a knowledgeable, willful act of design by its unknown mid-fifteenth-century designer.

1. Asymmetrical reading of left facade

2. Symmetrical center facade

3. Asymmetrical reading of right facade

4. "Regularized" version of the facade

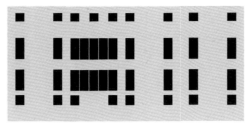

1. Multiple bay facade diagram

Multiple Bay Facades

The Venetian facade system composed exclusively of two bay types proved a remarkably flexible way of making larger, wider buildings. Apart from making double palazzi, the most common technique was by the addition of one or more side bays to a tripartite facade. An addition to one side only produced an asymmetrical facade, such as the Palazzo Priuli-Ruzzini in Campo Santa Maria Formosa, whereas an addition to both sides maintained the symmetry, as in the Palazzo Zenobio. Occasionally, another center bay would be added, as in the Palazzo Ferro-Fini.

2. Palazzo Pisani, begun early 17th c., finished 1728, by Girolamo Frigimelica

1. Palazzo Priuli-Ruzzini, begun ca. 1580, Bartolomeo Monopola

2. Palazzo Zenobio, late 17th c., Antonio Gaspari

1. Palazzo Fontana-Rezzonico, 16th c.

2. Palazzo Labia, begun ca. 1750, Alessandro Tremignon

1. Palazzo Surian-Bellotto, mid-17th c., Giuseppe Sardi

2. Palazzo Foscarini, second half of 16th c.

1. Palazzo Ferro-Fini, 17th c., Alessandro Tremignon

2. Palazzo Volpi di Misurata, 16th c.

1. Palazzo Zen, 16th c. with additions for three sons

2. Palazzo Zen, 16th c.

1. Casa d'Affitto (rental apartment building) at Campo San Basegio, 17th c.

2. Casa d'Affitto, view from Campo San Basegio

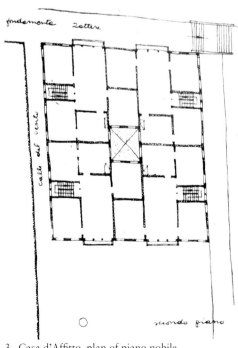

3. Casa d'Affitto, plan of piano nobile.

1. Palazzo of the Ghetto Nuovissimo on the rio degli Ormesini, 16th c.

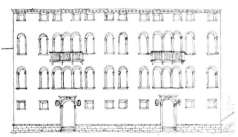

2. Elevation of Casa d'Affitto at Fondamenta Rossa

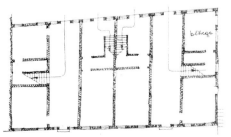

3. Plan of Casa d'Affitto at Fondamenta Rossa

Venezia Minore

In her book *Venezia Minore*, Egle Renata Trincanato points out that Venice had substantial rental housing as early as the twelfth and thirteenth centuries; this type of housing was designed using the same principles as the grand palaces. Much of this housing consisted of small units in series, *a schiera*, with simple facades—but several larger buildings are basically indistinguishable from larger palaces.

The apartment building at the Fondamenta Rossa is basically a double tripartite palazzo without the tracery, similar to the palazzo on the rio degli Ormesini above.

The San Basegio Casa d'Affitto has five bays rather than six, with two ingenious interlocking plans on the campo side and water side. The upper four floors are mirrored vertically to resemble a grand palazzo.

4. View from the Fondamenta Rossa

1. Palazzo on the Fondamenta Zattere at Ponte Lungo

2. Palazzo Foscari, 15th c.

Oddities

Many houses in Venice do not conform to the complete orthodoxy of the Venetian facade system. Of these anomalies, all are odd, some are ugly, some are banal, and some are very interesting. Some seem designed with intention, but others seem to have happened randomly. Somehow they are all forgiving and contribute to the quirky, eccentric quality of Venice—they blend in.

As stated previously, there are (almost) no examples of the traditional portego bay being used for one house—at least not a full, consistent one. The Palazzo Dandolo may be the only example.

Full of casual, shifting local symmetries, houses like the Palazzi Foscari, Morosini-Sagredo, and Minotto could almost be modern compositions.

3. Palazzo Donà della Madoneta, 13th c.

4. Palazzo Orio Semitecolo-Benzon, 14th c.

1. Palazzo Morosini-Sagredo, 14th c.

2. Palazzo Minotto, 15th c.

3. Palazzo Barbaro, 15th c.

4. Palazzo Dolfin, late 14th c.

5. Palazzo Dandolo, early 15th c.

6. Unknown palazzo

View of the Grand Canal

The City of Venice

Most architects have a hard time with Venice. It was not "planned." It does not have a nine-square grid plan like Jaipur. It is not based on a Roman Castrum or a cross-axial plan like so many European cities; Renaissance and Baroque urbanism did not appear in Venice; and it does not have nineteenth-century tree-lined boulevards or unified, rectangular urban squares. Its only defensive wall was an environmental one, and it had no fortress-like defensive buildings. In short, it is not Florence. But if it is not Florence, what is it? And, what are its lessons?

Venice was built incrementally, one building at a time, according to a very simple, seemingly rigid system of only two components: a side, blank bay and a central, open bay—a system that continued for centuries. This system was developed according to natural characteristics of the site, but it is far from natural. Beyond initial necessity, the city was the product of great will, pride, and judgment. The Istri-

an stone that gives Venice one of its primary characteristics had to be imported, as were all other building materials. Thus, Venice is an "artificial" city.

To counter the modern predilection for narcissistic and increasingly bizarre anti-urban architecture, many contemporary urbanists have championed the city composed of "Monuments and Urban Fabric," or alternatively, "Classical and Vernacular Architecture," implying that most of a city's architecture should be "background" architecture. Venice, however, demonstrates that urban fabric can be made of superb architecture throughout, no matter how small the building.

It is Venice's openness, and the astonishing variety and sophistication of its facades, that produce the mesmerizing beauty and character of the city. Florence is important—it gave us the Renaissance—but it is not beautiful. Venice is both important and beautiful, with rich lessons about architecture and urbanism.

View of the Grand Canal

The End of La Serenissima

Venice was an unconquered republic for eleven hundred years—from the first Doge in 697 until it succumbed to Napoleon in 1797. During this period, the Venetian facade had developed consistently for at least seven centuries, but this, too, ended with the end of the republic.

The end of the Venetian Republic and the end of the Venetian facade were not abrupt, however. The eighteenth century was, generally, a difficult period of economic and cultural decline for Venice. During this time, several churches and the La Fenice Opera were built, but only a few family palaces. Nevertheless, throughout the eighteenth century, Venice remained largely inoculated against outside influence, especially the profound architectural, urban, and philosophical changes occurring in France.

Except for a brief period as part of the Napoleonic Kingdom (1805–1814), Venice was ruled by Austria from 1797 to 1866, when it became part of Italy. There were some urban improvements under the Austrians, but Venice was essentially a complete city, impervious to new, straight streets and free-standing neoclassical buildings.

Urbanism and urban facade development waned in Venice during the eighteenth century. What continued, even increased, in other European cities followed neoclassical models, not Venetian models. Paris was especially important for the emphasis on intimacy and private life and for a completely new architectural relationship between the exterior and interior—the architectural promenade.

The Urban Facade Beyond Venice:
From the Grand Canal to the Grand Boulevard

The Architectural Promenade

The Venetian facade was the prelude to a wholly new relationship between the exterior and interior, developed by French theory and French practice in the eighteenth century—one that would only come to complete fruition, as the *promenade architecturale*, in the early twentieth century with the work of Le Corbusier.[1]

The architectural promenade is an experiential sequence of spaces, senses, and character, as an individual progresses through a work of architecture.

The germ of the idea is a sixteenth-century Italian inheritance that the French called an *appartement*—a simple group of three rectangular rooms: *antichambre, chambre, cabinet,* or waiting room, room, and study. This was a functional group but also a sequential group. During a time of no electronic communication, when both business and social transactions required in-person contact, this sequence had profound social and cultural importance. It was a sequence from public to private, around which increasingly elaborate social rituals were developed. For one person, the three-room *appartement* was a functional arrangement; for two or more people—visitor and visited—it had ritualistic connotations, regarding how far a visitor could penetrate into the more intimate rooms. This sequence was the primitive ancestor of the *promenade architecturale*, which really began in the early eighteenth century.

1. Hôtel de Matignon, Jean Courtonne, 1725

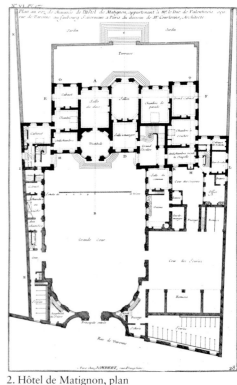

2. Hôtel de Matignon, plan

The architect Jean Courtonne's *Traité de perspective ... avec les remarques sur l'architecture*, published in 1725, was mostly devoted to perspective, with minimal, but important, remarks about architecture. One might ask why Courtonne devoted so much literary real estate to perspective, when perspective had been invented three hundred years earlier; perspective had revolutionized the architecture of the Renaissance by putting man at the center of the universe and of architecture, but it was not generally central to the idea of a spatial sequence. The answer lies in Courtonne's brief remarks on architecture.

Regular Exterior/Irregular Interior

Courtonne argued that symmetry is only necessary when it can be seen. In other words, the exterior of a building should be symmetrical, as should each of a variety of rooms, but not necessarily the plan, because it is not seen. Thus, his discourse on perspective takes on new meaning as individual perception in a sequence, or promenade.

Courtonne also argued for a *rapport parfait* between inside and out, but admitted that this is difficult and could only be achieved if the architect is an absolute master of his art. Courtonne's propositions were revolutionary, as they were based on human perception and sequence, not on abstract ideas of order. Implicitly, this was the birth of the *promenade architecturale*.

Courtonne's Hôtel de Matignon has both a variety of rooms and a perfect relationship between inside and outside, including the symmetrical re-centering between the forecourt and garden. Except for the round entry vestibule the rooms are regular and similar in size. As interiors became more complex, their relationship to a regular exterior became much more difficult to resolve.

Juste-Aurèle Messonier's Maison de Brethaus (1729–34) in Bayonne, for example, is a desperately difficult case. The discontinuity between the regularly spaced windows of the trapezoidal plan and the flamboyantly shaped rooms of the interior

is extreme. Given the problem, the adjustments are sophisticated.

As plans gradually became more and more figurative and flamboyant toward the middle of the eighteenth century, Pierre Patte, in 1769, complained that a structural problem was created because each floor was different, with discontinuous load-bearing walls. But this problem—the predecessor to the free-plan—would have to wait until the twentieth century and the invention of the columnar frame.

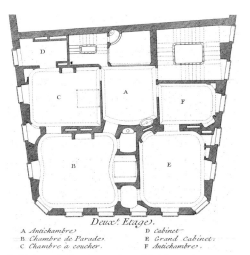

A *Antichambre*   D *Cabinet*
B *Chambre de Parade*   E *Grand Cabinet*
C *Chambre à coucher*   F *Antichambre*

1. Maison de Brethaus, plan, J-A Messonier, 1729–34

2. Maison de Brethaus, Bayonne

119

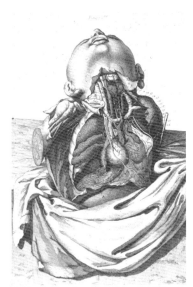

1. Engraving from the *Encyclopédie*

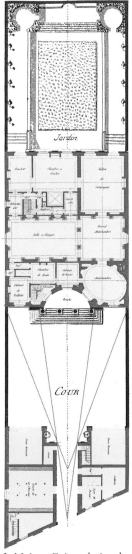

2. Maison Guimard, site plan

The mid-eighteenth century was an historical watershed. Diderot and d'Alembert's dictionary of rational knowledge, the *Encyclopédie*, began to be published in 1751, as architecture transformed from urban to free-standing suburban building types, interiors began to be more particularized, and the relationship between exterior and interior began to be considered as a sequence.

This was paralleled by interest in the human body. In fact, the *Encyclopédie* included a chapter on anatomy, in which the body was opened to reveal the internal functions.

In his 1780 treatise, Le Camus de Mézières argues that the outside and the inside of a building have "the most intimate relationship," and that it is the exterior that "prepares the spirit" by indicating the use of the building and what is to follow on the interior. His treatise also discussed an increased number of room types, their character, and color.

The Maison Guimard

Ledoux's 1770–72 house, known as the Temple of Terpsichore, was built for the first dancer of the Paris Opera, Mlle Marie-Madeleine Guimard. It is a clear manifestation of Le Camus's ideas. The iconography of the symmetrical facade, with its references to dance, belies the asymmetry of the interior, where Mlle Guimard's bath and bedroom are on axis but the public rooms are shifted asymmetrically off-axis. The house sequence, the *promenade architecturale*, begins at the *porte cochère*, under the theater, and ends in the garden.

The first view in the sequence was from the entry gate, with a framed view of the entry apse and its screen of four columns. Nearer the entry to the forecourt, a full view of the facade was revealed. After passing through the court, one entered the central bay of the columnar screen on axis, then entered the house diagonally into the oval *antichambre*, and then into the square *seconde antichambre*. From this room, one could pass through another four column screen (a recapitulation of the apse entry) into the dining room, or proceed directly through the center bay of four columns (another recapitulation) into the *salon de compagnie*, and finally into the garden.

3. Interior facade of second antichamber

4. Interior facade of dining room

5. Main Facade

6. Entry apse

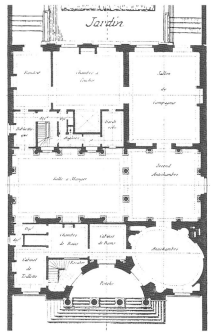

1. Maison Guimard plan, 1770–72

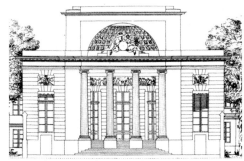

2. Facade drawing from Krafft and Ransonnette

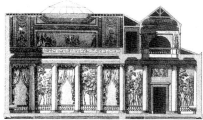

3. Section of dining room

The building's parti, *la distribution*, obviously has to do with the character of the owner, as well as her profession. Mlle Guimard was not only a famous dancer, she was an equally famous lover, supported by at least three different gentlemen. She was reputed to have given three dinner parties a week: one for the nobility, one for artists and intellectuals, and one for courtesans, as an orgy. Consequently, the distribution of the plan is Ledoux's architectural homage to the licentious owner.

The theater seated some five hundred people and was often used for performances too risque for the Paris Opera.

The dining room was covered in mirrors between the columns, with carved trees covering the joints and painted vegetation. The *salon de compagnie* had frescoes painted by Fragonard.

The bankruptcy of one of Mlle Guimard's lovers forced her to sell the house in 1786, which was destroyed in 1862, ironically due to the rearrangement of the streets around the site of Charles Garnier's new Paris Opera.

The architectural promenade and the role of the facade were central to the exploration of intimacy and private life in the late eighteenth century and a prelude to the extension of this exploration by Le Corbusier in the twentieth century.

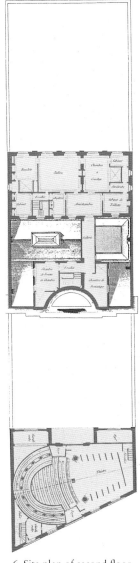

6. Site plan of second floor

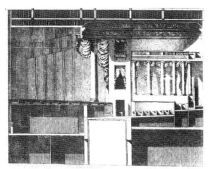

5. Theater section

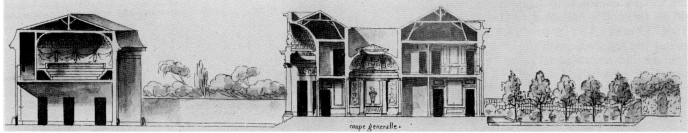

4. Long site section

1. Paris apartment buildings

2. Apartment house design from C. Daly

The Urban Promenade

As the population of cities increased in the nineteenth century, the apartment building and the street became the primary components of urbanism. This led to fresh importance of the urban facade.

Haussmann's boulevards in Paris were begun in 1853, and the facades were strictly regulated. Like the Venetian facade, Parisian ones were an exceptionally sophisticated type in mediating between private interiors and the social display of the boulevards. French windows (or doors) went all the way to the floor, behind transparent, shallow, so-called "French" balconies. This combination facilitated display and retreat along the boulevards.

By the late nineteenth century, the Parisian boulevard had become the urban model to emulate, as the street had become the primary instrument of urban design. The *promenade architecturale*—the architectural sequence—had emerged in the eighteenth century with neoclassical *hôtels* and the rise of individualism. In the nineteenth century this idea expanded to the developing public spaces of the city. Indeed, the Parisian boulevard, with its cafes, carriages, and street lights, became the theater of public life for the urban bourgeoisie—the setting for the *flâneur*, or *boulevardier*, and the *promenade urbaine*. During this period, Paris represented the pinnacle of public life for history's most expanded social class.

In America, this tradition continued until the city began to disintegrate after World War Two. The 1916 "step-back" zoning code in New York City bound architecture firmly to urban design just as the regulations of Paris's boulevards had done, and American architects were well-trained to design urban facades.

1. Family overlooking a boulevard, *The Balcony*, Édouard Manet, 1868

2. *Boulevard Haussmann*, Antoine Blanchard, 1970

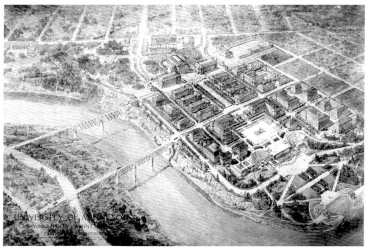

1. Plan for the University of Minnesota, Cass Gilbert, 1910

2. Rockefeller Center, New York, 1932–39

3. The Chrysler Building, William Van Alen, 1930

American Modernism 1890–1940

During the late nineteenth and early twentieth century there were virtually no modernist architects in America, but during this period of nation-building—the "American Renaissance"—American architects were knowledgeable and well-educated. A large percentage of the most prominent architects were trained at the École des Beaux-Arts in Paris. They could design a variety of building types, campus plans, urban plans, and urban architecture. They could do all of this while developing and exploiting complex modern building types and modern technology, such as the steel frame. The Chrysler building, for example, was all of these. It followed the 1916 "set-back" zoning code to define the street on the lower levels but became a skyscraper above. Classicism provided the knowledge base, but architects were gradually developing a genuinely modern language of urban architecture. Unfortunately, this ended with the Second World War, and the triumph of modernist architecture. An apropos question is: *How might American architecture have developed had it not been co-opted by one strain of European modernist architecture after the war?*

1. Aerial view of Place Vendôme, Paris, 1699

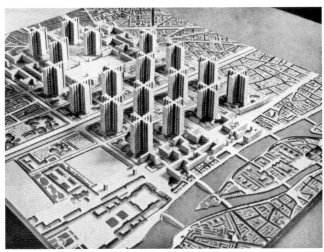

2. Model of Voisin Plan for Paris, Le Corbusier, 1925

European Modernism 1922–1940

History is full of watershed moments with dueling ideologies. In the early nineteenth century, for example, Ingres's classical painting, *Odalisque* (1814), could not be more different than Géricault's romantic painting, *Raft of the Medusa* (1818–19). This was only a difference of painting style and philosophy, however. But, even with hindsight, it is difficult to wrap one's mind around the implications of the publication of Hegemann and Peets's *American Vitruvius*, and Le Corbusier's *Ville Contemporaine*, in 1922.

This was a truly cataclysmic watershed moment. The *American Vitruvius*, with its promotion of Camillo Sitte and the traditional city as models for building a new nation, was totally dismissed by Le Corbusier and his anti-urban model for the city of towers.

Le Corbusier's architecture of the 1920s may have been embedded in the city, but his 1932 Porte Molitor apartment building was the last of that series. Otherwise, his work in the 1930s was marked by free-standing buildings and numerous modernist town planning schemes following the *Ville Contemporaine* model. His *Ville Radieuse* was published in 1933.

3. Glass skyscraper project, Mies van der Rohe, 1921

1. The Casa del Fascio, Como, 1932–36, Giuseppe Terragni

2. The Casa del Fascio

The Modern Facade

A central argument of this book has been that the (non-classical) Venetian facade provides ideas and inspiration for modern facades. Indeed, Le Corbusier—among the few modernist architects to make facades—owes a clear debt to Venice. For most modernists, however, the architectural facade was not a design consideration at all, and it remains a lost art for most contemporary architects. This is because modern architecture did not grow out of ideas about the city.

Two Strains of Modernism

Because it emerged in Europe in the early twentieth century, modern architecture has mostly been considered as a united movement—whether embraced or reviled. That said, there were two strains of early modern architecture: one growing out of Dutch de Stijl, German Rationalism, and Russian Constructivism, and the other growing out of Paris and Cubism.

The Amsterdam-Dessau-Moscow version of modernism believed in an absolute, unified view of the world—of continuity and "Total Design." Theo Von Doesburg, Hannes Meyer, and El Lissitzky promoted unified compositions of deep, diagonal space and isolated, anti-urban buildings. Axonometric drawings replaced five hundred years of perspective as a means of conveying architectural intent. This strain was, and is, incapable of urbanism.[1]

The Paris version of modernism, that of Le Corbusier, Alvar Aalto, and (perhaps) Giuseppe Terragni, believed in a more complex, discontinuous world. They promoted compositions of frontal, layered

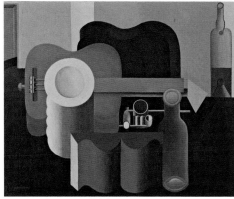

1. Le Corbusier, *Still life*, 1920

2. Reitveld and Von Doesburg, study, 1923

space and discontinuous, contrapuntal systems—a more complex view of architecture. Further, early works were embedded in the fabric of the traditional city. This strain was, and is, capable of urbanism.

Unfortunately, over time, the more simplistic version of modernism prevailed. European modernists began immigrating to America in the first half of the twentieth century, culminating with Mies going to IIT and Gropius going to Harvard in 1937. This was a major factor, among others, in the explosion of the more simplistic strain of modernism after World War Two.

For those interested in hypothetical architecture dinner party questions, a compelling one might be: What would modern American architecture have become if Le Corbusier rather than Walter Gropius, had gone to Harvard? Would a more complex, interesting American architecture have developed? Would architecture have continued to be related to the city? Would a more substantive, architectural knowledge base have continued?

Venetian Legacies

Long ago, Le Corbusier was linked to Palladio and Italian Mannerism by Colin Rowe, to the displeasure of many modernist architects and theoreticians.[2] By now it should be apparent that Le Corbusier also owes a great debt to Venice and the principles of figure/field and local symmetry.

First of all, Le Corbusier was almost alone among modernist architects in making facades. (A book of great modernist facades would be a very short book indeed.) And, although he utilized historical principles, his facades were made without the elements of historical architecture. He was obviously conversant with Palladio as well as Venice.

Palladio had also been familiar with the Venetian facade. Venetian architecture began to spread to the Italian mainland around the time Palladio was beginning to build. The side bay of the Venetian house facade, with its central blank panel, had had a long period of development, and it served as the basis for the Ca' Cogollo in Vicenza, which is attributed to Palladio, and also for Federico Zuccari's house in Florence. Like the Venetian bay, both the Ca' Cogollo and the Casa Zuccari had windows on the outer edges of the facade and a blank panel in the center of the facade.

Le Corbusier, also, was obviously intrigued by the blank central panel, as it appears in both his Villa Schwob and his Maison Plainex. His Villa at Garches, with its shifting local symmetries, also seems derived from Venetian models.

1. Structural wall of the Ca' Cogollo

2. Ca' Cogollo

3. Casa Zuccari, Florence

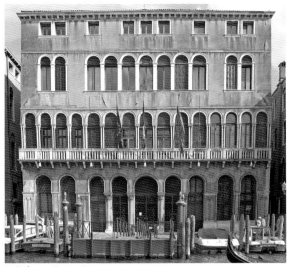

1. Palazzo Farsetti

2. Villa Stein

3. Villa Schwab

4. Maison Plainex

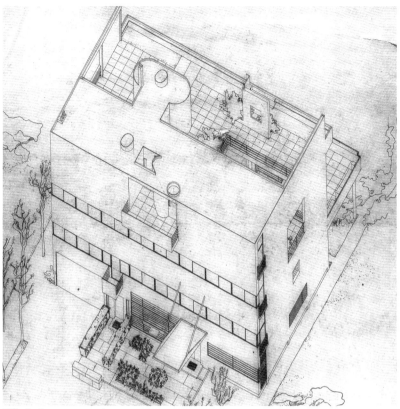

Villa Stein, axonometric

The Villa Stein-de-Monzie

The facade is not an important element of modernist architecture in general, and yet, after almost a century, the facade of Le Corbusier's Villa at Garches remains an astonishing masterpiece of the art of the facade—the equal of any historic or classical facade.

Strictly speaking, the Villa at Garches is not an urban building. It is referred to as a villa, not a town house (although it could have been a townhouse, like a grand French Hôtel). It is also not Le Corbusier's only modern urban facade; there are also the Maison Plainex, the Ozenfant studio, and the Villa Cook, among others.

The facade of Le Corbusier's villa at Garches has no suggestion of structural loads being carried to the ground—a distinctly un-classical idea. In his short, one-paragraph description of the 1927 project, Le Corbusier describes the structural frame, stating that it is independent, and that the facade no longer sits on the ground or supports the floors or the roof. He says that the facade is nothing more than a veil of glass and masonry enclosing the house. What he does not do is describe this "veil" as a facade. After deploying the columnar frame, there was no inherent reason to make a facade, yet Le Corbusier made one nevertheless—a wall, a surface, a picture plane.

The facade of the Villa at Garches exhibits all of the problems and principles of "The Facade," thereby relating to the issues of non-classical Venetian facades. Unlike Venetian facades, which act as mediators between the public and private realms, the facade of the Villa at Garches is a membrane. Nevertheless, the principles through which one can read and understand Venetian facades apply equally to the facade at Garches. Namely, frontality, figures and fields, transparency, symmetry, asymmetry, local symmetries, proportion, literal and phenomenal depth, and vertical and horizontal integration. Le Corbusier's facade could have been a banal example of stylistic abstraction, but it has been charged and activated by these design principles.

1. Villa Stein

2. Villa Stein without three-dimensions

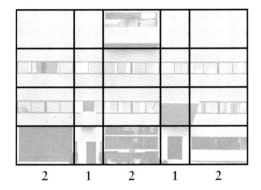

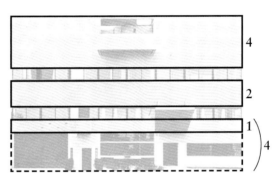

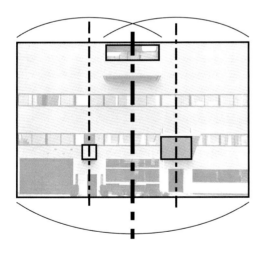

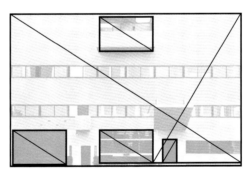

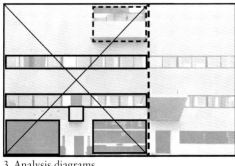

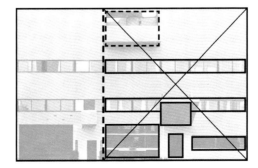

3. Analysis diagrams

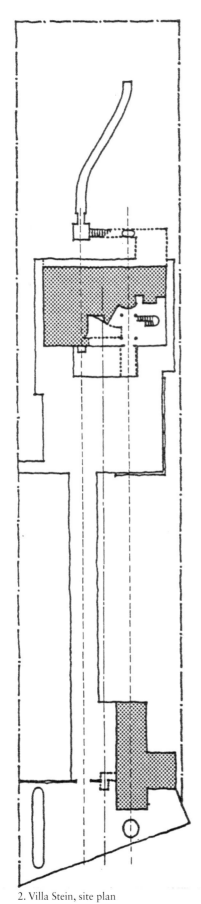

2. Villa Stein, site plan

1. Villa Stein, view from entry

3. Villa Stein, left three bays of the facade

2. Interior view behind facade

1. Villa Stein, view from forecourt

Symmetry, Frontality, and Depth

The Villa at Garches is located far back on a long, rectangular site. From the entrance gate, it is possible to see the facade only frontally—but not along the central axis, as the entry drive is centered on the left three bays of the facade. From this distance, the dark panels of the garage and central ground floor window appear as dark caverns flanking the small balcony and service entrance. As one moves closer, the three left bays form an apparently complete frontal facade that is primarily asymmetrical, but that re-centers about the small, central bay. It is not possible to see the overall symmetry of the facade, because the center axis is blocked by landscape, making the complete facade impossible to see by foot or car except along the minor axis.

As one arrives at the motor court in front of the house, the facade turns to a slightly oblique, rather than frontal view. This reveals the overall symmetry of the facade, as well as the three-dimensional aspect of the picture plane's three projections (two balconies and entrance canopy) and the literal depth of the opening to the terrace on the top floor.

Because there is no representation of structural loads carried to the ground,

the facade reads like a taut membrane, stretched laterally to the edges. The ribbon windows cut clearly through the opaque surface on either side of the facade, so that the vertically graduated ribbons of surface appear to float, or even to pass transparently behind the glass.

Thus, despite the abstraction of the facade, the picture plane is remarkably agitated by symmetry, frontality, and depth.

3. Villa Stein, oblique view

The Free Plan

The Villa is based on a contrapuntal system of a rational structural grid and a relative array of figural space and objects. The design provides a sequence of alternating frontal and oblique tableaux as one progresses through the house on a *promenade architecturale*.

The Architectural Promenade

Stepping into the house, one pauses in a horizontal layer of space—like a thick wall—before stepping into a rectangular space defined by four rounded columns. This space, reminiscent of Laugier's primitive hut or the columns of a Tuscan atrium, acts together with the plane of the facade as a stabilizing figure for the surrounding curvilinear composition. Several (four or five?) frontal layers of space are defined with a convex curve on axis with the entry and framed perspectively by a diagonal wall and the vertical diagonal of the stair. One then moves obliquely to the stair, to move up in the concavity of the curve of the stair.

Emerging on the piano nobile, one arrives perpendicular to the entry axis (or Tuscan atrium) below. The rail of the stair opening peels out of the large terrace window, which is identical to the central ground floor window between entrances. The curved parapet/bookcase shifts the path diagonally, to reveal the convex curve of the dining room framed by two columns, in a perpendicular recapitulation of the ground floor tableaux.

The path then shifts perpendicular to the central axis of the building into the living "room," which extends all the way through the house. From here, the space opens up to the garden through large, double-height ribbon windows. From this space, one can pass parallel to the facade into the dining room and, thus, the concave side of the curved wall. Or, conversely, one can return to the curvilinear parapet/bookcase, from where one can access the double-height terrace and go into the garden, or access the stair to the roof terrace overlooking the garden.

1. Villa Stein, facade

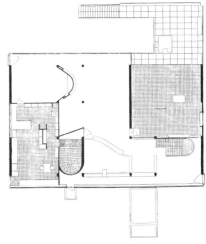
2. Second floor plan

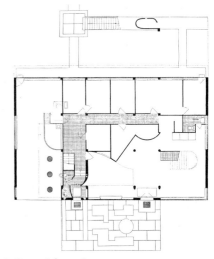
3. Ground floor plan

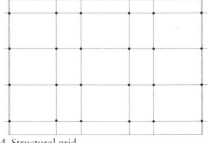
4. Structural grid

1. View to living room

2. Terrasse

3. View of library

4. View inside facade

5. View of entry hall

6. View from back of stair

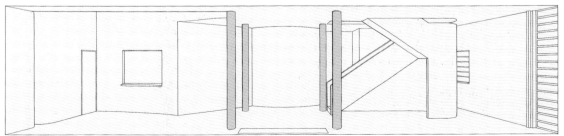

7. Perspective view from entry

1. Ozenfant Studio, 1922, urban context

2. Maison Plainex, 1927, urban context

3. Le Corbusier in Venice

4. Maison Plainex, facade

1. Port Molitor, 1931–34, urban context

2. Chandigarh Secretariet, 1958

Le Corbusier in Urban Context

Le Corbusier's early work was carefully embedded and related to the traditional urban fabric of Paris. Published images of the work in Le Corbusier's highly influential *Oeuvre Complète 1920–1929* were severely cropped, however, presumably to make the projects appear more abstract and revolutionary—as polemical examples of the International Style.

The facade of the Maison Plainex, for example, is shown only in a cropped, frontal view without context. In actuality, the "blank panel" of the facade is a projection that helps negotiate the differences in alignment of the two adjacent party wall buildings.

Likewise, the Ozenfant Studio is shown cropped and devoid of context. In reality, it anchors the corner between a major urban street and a diagonal neighborhood street on axis with the spiral stair and the cubic studio. The building has been significantly altered, so it is not possible to obtain a photo of the original context. (The image shown here is a Photoshop reconstruction.)

The Porte Molitor apartment building was also shown in isolation. In reality, the building is one of a series of party wall buildings that originally overlooked a large sports park of athletic fields, a situation which Le Corbusier described as related to the *Ville Radieuse.*

These early works held great promise, both architecturally and urbanistically. The architecture was complex and contextually sophisticated. Had Le Corbusier's urbanism been equal to his architecture, the world might be a richer place today. Unfortunately, however, his urbanism followed the principles of the more simplistic strain of modernism—the deep space, isolated, anti-urban architecture of Walter Gropius, Theo Von Doesburg, Hannes Meyer, and others. When this strain became dominant, it resonated with corporate America via Gropius's Graduate School of Design at Harvard, and spread like an international virus. The truth is, it might not have made a difference if Le Corbusier, rather than Gropius, had gone to Harvard.

But if America is to develop a truly urban architecture to reconstruct American towns and cities, Le Corbusier's early architecture—and Venice—provides ample principles.

1. Prudential Center, Boston, C. Luckman, 1964

2. Central Boston, red areas demolished under "Urban Renewal," 1950s–60s

Apocalypse

European modernist architects began arriving in America in the 1930s to teach and practice. Aligned with Le Corbusier's CIAM strategies of (non) urbanism, Walter Gropius's arrival at the Harvard design program in 1937 promoted the simplistic strain of modernism, and it exploded with apocalyptic success in America after the Second World War. Indeed, for decades the Harvard Graduate School of Design was the East Coast distributor of anti-urban architecture.

By the end of the Second World War in 1945, the revolution outlined in 1922 came to fruition. The "American Renaissance" disappeared into the past; the professional education system of the École des Beaux-Arts was reviled as the enemy and disappeared from American professional schools; corporate America discovered the economic benefits of the war's industrial advances, as well as the clarity and iconic benefits of buildings detached from their urban context. The future had finally arrived. Cities began to unravel as the automobile became the tool for suburban freedom. Urbanism responded with *Urban Renewal*. Architecture responded with simplistic versions of the Dutch, German, and Russian strain of modernism.

The facade, no longer germane, was replaced by the glass curtain wall. Terms like "skin" and "envelope" replaced "facade." Gradually, building shapes became increasingly idiosyncratic to feed ever increasing architectural and client egos. The long-standing balance between civic responsibility and private prerogative was replaced by the hegemony of the private realm. Architecture became privatized.

3. Postwar advertisement

1. Dancing Towers, D. Libeskind

2. Dubai

Contemporary Modernism

It is too soon for a history of early-twenty-first-century architecture, but even a cursory review of contemporary architecture reveals that the most talented architects are still absorbed with crafting the architectural object rather than architectural space, much less urban space. Digital technology has furthered this quest. Most buildings and projects are isolated, self-absorbed objects floating in space, with few, if any, urban implications. Elaborately warped envelopes have replaced the faceted surfaces of machine-age buildings, but the anti-urban characteristics of most contemporary architecture are at least as strong, if not more so, than those of the early-twentieth-century modernists.

Parametric modeling, for all its sex appeal, has become the architectural opioid of the twenty-first century—a highly seductive and addictive distraction.

The twenty-first century will be the century of the environment and the city, but it is not yet clear what digital technology's positive contribution might be.

3. Project, Z. Hadid

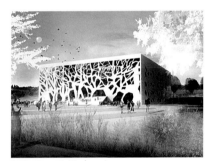

4. Project, B. Tschumi

5. Project, ZHA

6. Housing project, MVRDV

1. Project in China

2. Westermoskee, Amsterdam

Architecture and the City

In the early twenty-first century there are again two strains of modernism. They parallel those of the early twentieth century.

One grows out of the simplistic, anti-urban strain of early modernism—the Amsterdam-Dessau-Moscow strain. The contemporary version of this strain is completely self- and media-absorbed. Often favored by talented architects, this strain shuns urban relationships in the quest for ever more shocking architectural forms.

The other strain believes in a more complex architecture—one that is an embedded component of urbanism. This strain requires a knowledge base about the long tradition of architecture and the city, which includes the knowledge and ability to design urban facades. In contrast to the "me, me, me" narcissism of most contemporary architecture, there have been major efforts to rediscover the city and architecture's relationship to it for at least half a century, but this effort is not yet a dominant force. Education is at least partly to blame. Urbanism is rarely taught in architecture schools, and students are left to overdose on sexy digital imagery without context or knowledge base.

The future of humanity and cities is arguably uncertain due to environmental issues, but if there is to be a future, it will have to be urban, as cities are the most ecologically efficient form of human settlements.

A basic question is: Can a modern architectural language be developed to produce beautiful, livable, sustainable cities? I believe the answer is yes, but it will require the reorientation of architecture to engage the city. Object buildings can make statistical cities, but not urban ones. Urban buildings are required, and urban buildings require facades.

The Venetian facade is a high level of architectural achievement without the need for further justification or purpose. It may again provide important lessons for contemporary architecture, however. For over seven hundred years, a simple two-part Venetian facade typology provided endless flexibility, interpretation, and variation, one in which artistic excellence was achieved within the system, not by defying the system to get attention.

1. Fantasy street of object buildings

2. Amsterdam, Jordan

3. Ithaca, New York, State Street

4. Venice, Grand Canal

"… always start with the pics."

Pictures and Words

Many years ago, arriving back in the United States and beginning to teach at Cornell after five years in Europe, I received the following succinct advice from Colin Rowe, "Michael, … always start with the pics." This is very good advice for architects, because while literature is about words and ideas, architecture is about *form* and ideas.

It was an education watching Colin prepare a lecture. He always began with one or two slides on a small, vertical sorting tray. He would then contemplate the slide, or slides, for what sometimes seemed like an inordinately long time. Then, at some point, another slide would appear, either before, between, or after—usually between or after, because the first slide was the ethical agent precipitating the exploration of ideas to follow. Gradually, more slides were added, with continual rearrangement. No notes were ever taken, but when the lecture hall lights went off, the voice of the oracle from the darkness was well-rehearsed, enabling novice minds to enter and roam freely among complex subject matter. In revealing their ideas, inanimate objects—whether friends or frenemies—became energized in inspirational ways; and comparative and contradictory examples engendered both fervent belief and, often, equally fervent doubt.

Layout of Text and Images

Historically, architectural treatises by architects, such as those by Serlio, Du Cerceau, Palladio, and others, consisted mostly of engraved plates of drawings and little to no text. Until the nineteenth century, treatises were printed on archival paper, so a first edition Serlio from 1550 is still as sharp and clear today as it was originally.

Until the printing of color images embedded within the text became technically and economically feasible in the late twentieth century, the printing of architecture books was terrible. Images were either grouped separately from the text (as plates) on glossier paper, or they were mungy black and white images, often across the gutter, cropped badly, or without parallax correction. They were also too often separated by several pages from their descriptive text. This is because, typically, authors give book text and images separately to a publisher, and the book designer tries to get the images "as close as possible" to the relevant text. Even today book designers seem to have no problem running the images across the gutter, or not adjusting for parallax. Text and images belong together, however.

Venetian Facade Images

Architecture and urban knowledge is best obtained by first-hand experience in person—not from books, but from the real thing. An old German proverb says it best: the eyes believe themselves, the ears believe other people.

This is especially true of Venice. My first visit to Venice, almost sixty years ago, was a humbling experience—a challenge to everything I had known until then. I have been back many times since, but most of the images for this study were made over the last few years. Camera technology has improved enormously, but Adobe Photoshop and ON1 Photo RAW are still crucial for the many required image adjustments; foremost among these are straightening, cutting and pasting, object removal, de-noising, sharpening, color adjustments, and sometimes sky replacement. This is very time consuming.

Perspective and Frontality

One often hears it said, "Oh, proportions only work when they are seen front-on." This is completely incorrect, however. Facades "work," and can be appreciated, both obliquely and frontally. The facade of the Casa Cogollo in Vicenza is a case in point—one of many that is usually seen obliquely. Frontal views can achieve both literal and phenomenal depth via layering, superimposition, and perspective. This can be appreciated frontally, but slightly oblique views can also be very powerful, as in Marion Mahony Griffin's remarkable perspectives of Frank Lloyd Wright's early work.

Like paintings, facades can only be designed frontally—in elevation—as this is the purest view, and the easiest to manipulate. This is why the Venetian facades in this study are presented frontally. More importantly, this is the way most Venetian facades are intended to be seen. They are independent, ideal elements, even when they are party wall buildings.

There are many picturesque examples of Venetian facades in context, but they were not designed that way, or for that purpose. They are thus not "contextual" in the sense of having been designed for a particular context. This is why there are few contextual views in this study. Both symmetrical and asymmetrical Venetian facades are autonomous. In fact, the mesmerizing beauty of Venice derives from the cacophonous juxtaposition of this endless variety of sizes, shapes, and styles of facades, but with traditional facade typologies and similar traditional components, such as windows, balconies, etc., both consistency and variety are thereby enhanced.

1. Casa Cogollo, Vicenza, attributed to Palladio

2. Frontal view of Casa Cogollo

143

Notes

'Veneziani Gran Signori'

1. These are the first four lines of a traditional rhyme about the differing character of the cities of the Veneto region of Italy. It was originally in Veneto dialect and is at least five hundred years old. Consequently, there are many interpretations and variations even in Italian. It is impossible to make a literal translation into English, especially of the terms *Dottore* and *Signori*. *Dottore* means "doctor" in English, but almost always "medical doctor," whereas in Italy it almost always means a "university graduate," and is used like a title. (Even a notary public is referred to with the title *Notaio*.) Normally, *signore* simply means "mister," "sir," or "gentleman," and *signori* is the plural. *Signori* can have a more elevated significance, however, especially when it is *Gran Signori*, which is usually translated as "great lords," "gentlemen," "aristocrats," or "nobles"—none of which are exactly correct in English. The rhyme, with *Gran Signori*, is used in this study because in the sixteenth century, Venetians and Vicentines had pretensions of being descendants of the ancient Romans. For example, after the Gothic loggia of Vicenza's Basilica collapsed in the sixteenth century, Giulio Romano advised rebuilding the Gothic loggia. This would not have connected Vicenza to its supposed Roman past, so Andrea Palladio, protégé of the humanist Gian Giorgio Trissino, was selected to rebuild the loggia in the classical style—even though this was at least fifty years out-of-date by that point. Classicism also began to flourish in Venice during the same period.

    An English approximation of the rhyme might be:

    > *Venetians great lords, or nobles*
    > *Paduans great teachers, or intellectuals*
    > *Vicentines cat-eaters, or eat cats*
    > *Veronese all mad, or crazy*

2. See M. Dennis, "Classicism and the City," *ANTA: Archives of New Traditional Architecture*, Vol. 1, 108–127, ed. R. Economakis and M. Mesko (Notre Dame: University of Notre Dame School of Architecture, 2021).
3. See T. Schumacher, "The Skull and the Mask: The Modern Movement and the Dilemma of the Facade," *The Cornell Journal of Architecture: The Vertical Surface* 3 (1988), 4–11.
4. See C. Rowe, "Chicago Frame," *The Mathematics of the Ideal Villa and Other Essays* (Cambridge: MIT Press, 1976) 89–109, First published in the *Architectural Review*, 1956.
5. I am indebted to Jim Tice for pointing this out as I had never seen this room.
6. Rowe, "Chicago Frame."

Venezia: *Forma Urbis*

1. For the form and development of Venice, see G. Perocco, *Civiltà di Venezia*, Vol. 1 (Venezia: Stamperia di Venezia, 1977).
2. Perocco, *Civiltà di Venezia*.
3. For the development of the Piazza San Marco, see Foscari, 12–27; also, Parrott.

Venezia: *Forma Urbis*

1. The comparison of the Palazzo Medici-Riccardi and the Doge's Palace is owed to Colin Rowe's Renaissance lectures at Cornell in 1969.
2. For an analysis of classical layered facades, see T. Schumacher, "The Palladio Variations," *The Cornell Journal of Architecture: The Vertical Surface* 3 (1988), 12–29.
3. See Schumacher, "Palladio."

Venetian Facade

1. See A. von Hildebrand, *Das Problem der Form in der Bildenden Kunst* ("The Problem of Form in Painting and Sculpture"), first published in 1893.

2. See, C. Rowe, and R. Slutzky, "Transparency: Literal and Phenomenal," *The Mathematics of the Ideal Villa and Other Essays* (Cambridge: MIT, 1976) 158–183. Written, 1955–56. First published in *Perspecta*, 1963.
3. The term figure/field is used here in lieu of figure/ground because it is a better representation of the characteristics of facades. "Ground" is too simple a term for the relationship with figures. "Field" implies a fabric, which contains figures in a reciprocal, fluctuating relationship, not a simple contrasting one.
4. These are "fantasy" facades, i.e., facades of actual buildings that have been digitally adjusted to fit the Casa Correr facade.
5. For details of the construction of the facade of the Ca' D'Oro, see, Howard, 103–106.
6. The color collages were done by Cornell architecture students during a study of the Ca' D'Oro.

The Urban Facade Beyond Venice

1. For material in this section, see M. Dennis, *Court & Garden: From the French Hôtel to the City of Modern Architecture* (Cambridge: MIT Press, 1986).

The Modern Facade: *Problems and Principles*

1. See Rowe and Slutzky, "Transparency."
2. See Rowe, *Mathematics*.

Glossary

albergo meeting room in a *scuola*

altana roof platform of a Venetian house

androne large ground floor hall

calle narrow street

campo square (literally field)

canale canal

casa house

ca' house in Venetian dialect

casa fondaco house with ground floor business

doge chief magistrate of Venetian Republic

fondamenta waterside street

maison house

messá mezzanine

modenatura a dente dental molding

nuove new, plural

palazzo palace

piano nobile principal living floor

pianterrano ground floor

piazza square

portego large hall on living floors

procuratie managers of St. Mark

promenade architecturale architectural sequence

proto architect in charge of public buildings

rio canal

rio terrà filled canal

riva waterside street

sala room

salizzada paved street

salone large room

scuola guild or confraternity

serliana three bay window with center arch

sestiere district or neighborhood

sottoportego passageway under a building

strada nuova new street

terrazzo composite stone flooring

tondo circular panel or window

traghetto gondola ferry

vecchie old, plural

zecca mint

References

This is intended to be a minimal list of bibliographical references. One reason is that many of the sources cited below have extensive bibliographies. Another, more important reason is that this book, as stated in the preface, is not about history or theory. Nor is it a guidebook. It is about architecture, urbanism, design, and the Venetian facade. Thus, the most important resource is personal experience of the city of Venice. Facts of history may provide useful light, but there is no substitute for personal observation and recording.

BASSI, E. *Palazzi di Venezia*. Venice: La Stamperia di Venezia, 1976.

CONCINA, E. *A History of Venetian Architecture*. Cambridge: Cambridge, 1998.

FOSCARI, G. *Elements of Venice*. Zurich: Lars Meuller, 2014.

FRANZOI, U., AND M. SMITH. *The Grand Canal*. New York: Rizzoli, 2001.

GOY, G. H. *Venetian Vernacular Architecture: Traditional Housing in the Venetian Lagoon*. Cambridge: Cambridge, 1989.

———. *Venice: The City and its Architecture*. London: Phaidon, 1997.

HOWARD, D. *The Architectural History of Venice*. New Haven: Yale, 2002.

———. *Jacopo Sansovino: Architecture and Patronage in Renaissance Venice*. New Haven: Yale, 1975

LANE, F. C. *Venice: A Maritime Republic*. Baltimore: Johns Hopkins, 1973.

LAURITZEN, P., AND A. ZIELCKE. *Palaces of Venice*. New York: Viking, 1978.

LORENZETTI, G. *Venice and its Lagoon: Historical Artistic Guide*. Trieste: Lint, 1961.

MADDEN, T. F. *Venice: A New History*. New York: Penguin, 2012.

MARETTO, P. *La Casa Veneziana nella storia della città dalle origini all'Ottocento*. Venice: Marsilio, 1986.

NORWICH, J. J. *A History of Venice*. New York: Knopf, 1982.

PARROTT, D. *The Genius of Venice: Piazza San Marco and the Making of the Republic*. New York: Rizzoli, 2013.

PEROCCO, G., and A. SALVADORI. *Civiltà di Venezia*. Vol 1, *Le origini e il Medeo Evo*. Venice: Stamperia di Venezia, 1973.

———. *Civiltà di Venezia*. Vol 2, Il Rinascimento. Venice: Stamperia di Venezia, 1974.

POLLI, V. *Mauro Codussi: Architetto Bergamasco, 1440?–1504*. Bergamo: Bolis, 1993.

PUPPI, L. *Michele Sanmicheli: Architetto di Verona*, Padua: Marsilio, 1971.

RESINI, D. *Venice: The Grand Canal*. Treviso: Vianello, 2004.

SALZANO, E. *Atlante di Venezia: La forma della città in scala 1:1000 nel fotopiano enella carta numerica*. Venice: Comune di Venezia/Marsilio, 1989.

TOURING CLUB ITALIANO. *Venezia e dintorni*. Milan, 1951.

TRINCANATO, E. R. *Venezia Minore*. Venice: Filippi, 1948.

Index

Illustrations

Every effort has been made to contact copyright holders, but should there be any errors or omissions, the publisher would be pleased to insert the acknowledgment in any subsequent edition of this book.

Illustrations not listed below are either by the author, or in the public domain.

A. Chimacoff 141.3; ARS 11.1-2, 127.1, 129.2-4, 130, 131.1-2, 132.2-3, 133.1-3, 134.1-3, 135.1-6, 136.1-4, 137.1, 125.2; Google 12, 13, 17.4, 20.2, 24.3, 25.2, 26.2, 27.2, 28.2, 29.2-3, 139.2, 140.2; D. Descouens CC BY-SA 4.0 29.4; ZHA 139.3, 139.5; T. Hisgett 16.6, CC BY-SA 2.0; D. Liebeskind 139.1; C. Luckman 138.1; M. van der Rohe 11.3, 125.3; W. Mordoer CC BY-SA 2.5 46.2, 47.2; MVRDV 139.6; G. Perocco, Civiltá 14.2, 15, 18; G. Reitveld 127.2; B. Tschumi 139.4; vanupied 45.2; wga.hu 8.3.